Merseyside Special Investment Fund

SOLICITORS

BIBBY
FINANCIAL SERVICES

the mersey
PARTNERSHIP

midascapital
Midas Capital Partners Limited

theobjectiveoneprogramme
eu&merseyside
European Funding is Creating New Opportunities

the culture of capital

of capital

make your fortune on Merseyside by 2008

by
Arabella McIntyre-Brown

CAPSICA

the culture of capital

Written by Arabella McIntyre-Brown
Glossary and sourcebook compiled by Fiona Shaw
Technical advice: Antonia Potter
Cover design: Ken Ashcroft
Photographs on pages 5, 12-13, 17, 28, 30-31, 48 by Guy Woodland
Printed and bound in Spain by Bookprint SL

ISBN 0-9548431-0-X

First published in 2005 by Capsica
Capsica Ltd
83 Ampthill Road
Liverpool L17 9QN
www.capsica.net

Acknowledgements

Huge thanks to everyone who made this book possible, especially to Steve Stuart, whose imagination and energy brought the project together and drove it forward. I'm most grateful to the sponsors: Bibby Factors NW, Business Liverpool, DWF, Government Office Merseyside, Merseyside Special Investment Fund, Midas Capital, The Mersey Partnership. Thanks also to the Liverpool Culture Company and Liverpool City Council for their enthusiastic support and endorsement. And to the following people, my thanks for invaluable help, support and guidance: Mark Basnett, Simon Edwards, Jon Else, John Flamson, Suzanne Fulton, Jason Harborow, David Hinder, Nichola Lee, Geraldine McEntegart, Chris Musson, Larry Neild, Antonia Potter, Angela Smith, Mike Storey, Mike Taylor, David Wade-Smith, Phil Whitehurst. And, of course, to the Capsica team, as ever.

For information on events and more books in the Culture of Capital series, go to www.cultureofcapital.com

contents

7 Foreword and introduction

12 CHAPTER 1: Capital of enterprise culture
Business in the context of Merseyside

30 CHAPTER 2: Making it
A corporate finance primer for ambitious entrepreneurs

86 CHAPTER 3: Picking a winner
Current and future business leaders

96 Jargon

104 Getting help

This book was born out of frustration. So much was happening in and around Liverpool — exciting stuff that we d all been longing for. But great chunks of the city were still not connecting. People whinging about what they thought they ought to be getting but weren t. Other people grousing about life being unfair, and certain factions moaning about various other factions.

And this added to the constant aggravation of having the whole of the business community perceived so negatively by a large percentage of the world. One lot thinks that profit is inherently evil, another lot thinks business is dry and dull.

Dull? People, their dreams and passions, and money — it s the stuff of high drama, for heaven s sake. And as for profit — it has no moral properties. It s how you make it and what you do with it that matters.

Anyway — the book. This is not a technical guide to business finance, there are few statistics, and some major issues are given the lightest airing, needing far more space than this book can provide.

The point is to make you think about the possibilities for your business (whether or not it yet exists) with an open mind.

It shows you the dream, and shows you some of the nightmares, too. Few things that are worth having are easily come by, but you should at least know what lies within your grasp, if you reach for it.

Arabella McIntyre-Brown

The next five years, leading up to and beyond Liverpool s year as European Capital of Culture, offer local entrepreneurs the greatest business opportunity in 40 years.

But we aren t waiting for 2008 to roll round: 2005 is the year of the sea: Sea Liverpool promises enormous potential in this most maritime of cities. Liverpool s fortune was floated in on the Mersey tide, created in the wake of ships sailing to every ocean, every great river, in pursuit of trade.

Global trade may work very differently these days, but the world still comes here. At the Liverpool Culture Company we are besieged with proposals and offers from companies all over the world, eager to get involved in the year-long festival and the next three years of events leading up to Liverpool s 800th birthday in 2007 and 2008 itself. It s wonderful to see Liverpool attracting such keen attention from all corners of the globe, but we want to see more expressions of interest from local businesses. There is money to be made in every sector, and for every size of business. An important part of the benefits of winning the Culture title is the huge boost it will give to the local economy.

I am delighted to offer my enthusiastic support to this excellent and enterprising Culture of Capital project, and look forward to seeing many new entrepreneurs leaping to the challenge.

Jason Harborow, Liverpool Culture Company

An entrepreneurial approach to boosting the enterprise culture

If we are to see a resurgence of the private sector in this historically enterprising city and its neighbouring boroughs, there is only one approach to take; one mindset to adopt. We — the public and private sector individuals and organisations offering support, advice and backing to entrepreneurs — must be entrepreneurial ourselves, or why should they take any notice?

We have to get the message out to business owner managers, to ambitious business start ups, to energetic undergraduates, to those naturally enterprising employees who have never thought about running their own business. We need to break down the fear of the unknown, the myths and misconceptions, and inject a little excitement into the potential for business in and around Liverpool.

So the team behind this book have seized the opportunity and are planning a series of events and publications backed up by original in-depth research into the local SME base.

As capital markets develop, there is more money chasing fewer opportunities, but ironically it is no easier to raise investment. Gap funding has become an art in itself. One welcome intervention is the emergence of public sector backed funds that are aimed at the small firms gap. This region has the Merseyside Special Investment Fund, the North West Equity Fund, the Rising Stars Fund and others.

The restructuring of the region s business support network and a renewed sense of energy and commitment in the public sector focused on enterprise is all to be applauded and given enthusiastic backing. But it s not enough. It s certainly not the sole responsibility of the public sector. Entrepreneurs must accept the challenge and crack on, not wait for someone to hand them a prize on a plate. And the professional and financial community must invest in finding the potential stars, and help owner-managers transform into entrepreneurs.

This whole project sprang from a conversation with a business journalist — the author of this book. But a good idea is nothing without backing, and our team of sponsors needed little persuasion to help make it happen.

So spread the word — use this book and help bring in a new Age of Enterprise on Merseyside.

Steve Stuart
The Steve Stuart Partnership

chapter 1
Capital of
enterprise culture

300 years

Rivers and oceans provide a wealth of images, from trade winds to tides, to illustrate changing fortunes. The Mersey, with its enormous 30 ft range from high to low tide, its ever-changing channels and sandbanks and the speed of its tidal race, is a rich metaphor for Liverpool.

For more than 300 hundred years, Liverpool has exerted huge influence over the world's trade, transport and commerce. Inventive, brave, enterprising, visionary, ambitious – this city has bred or attracted people who wanted to make their fortune and change history. There are lists of famous individuals: Laird, Rathbone, Hornby, Gladstone, Vestey, Cunard – world beaters, all of them.

But there are their peers and equals who are almost forgotten – Liverpool entrepreneurs today need to know about these astonishing people and what they achieved. Don't let's rest on our historic laurels, but do let's be inspired by these entrepreneurial role models and breathe the spirit of enterprise back into the city.

Bryan Blundell, mariner, dock master, writer, philanthropist, founded the Bluecoat School in 1709; the remarkable William Hutchinson was a privateer (state-licensed pirate) then became Liverpool's dockmaster in 1759, inventing tide tables, establishing the world's first lifeboat station at Formby, writing books on naval architecture, and working out how to resuscitate people who were drowning. Endlessly inventive and enterprising.

The start of the passenger railway here may be well known, and George Stephenson's name famous, like that of his locomotive Rocket. But who remembers Henry Booth, who pushed the huge railway project through from idea to fruition, inventing things in his spare time? And Thomas Brassey, Birkenhead born in 1805, who was the greatest railway contractor in the world, building railways from Canada to India.

Say 'cooperative' and most people think 'Rochdale Pioneers'; but the Liverpool Cooperative Society was formed 15 years earlier.

The Vestey brothers, sent by their father – owner of Liverpool butcher's shops – to Argentina to find new opportunities; they founded the Blue Star shipping line.

Sir Alfred Lewis Jones, who owned Elder Dempster, opened up trade on the West African coast, imported the first bananas into Britain, founded the Liverpool School of Tropical Medicine (world's first). Alfred and Philip Holt designed and built their Blue Funnel ships which dominated trade in the Far East for decades.

Cotton, rubber, sugar, wheat, palm oil – these built Liverpool fortunes and fed industry throughout Britain.

And of course there were the entrepreneurs that Liverpool sent abroad – none more extraordinary than Robert Morris, financier of the American Revolution. But that's a story for another day.

Henry Tate's global sugar empire – Tate & Lyle – was based in Liverpool for over 100 years

James Muspratt, John Brunner and Ludwig Mond, all chemists based in Liverpool, were three of the four cornerstones of the chemicals giant ICI

Sebastian de Ferranti, born in Bold Street, Liverpool, was an electrical engineering genius, taking out 176 patents in his lifetime. Ferranti was the biggest company of its kind in the world, until the 1990s

1,000 years in Europe

When Britain was at war with bits of Europe from time to time, Liverpool mariners became privateers and captured French and Spanish prizes, under licence from the Crown.

The Wirral coast is second only to Cornwall in its long history of wrecking ships and smuggling brandy, silk, tobacco under the noses of the Revenue men.

For six months over the winter of 1912/13, Adolf Hitler stayed in Toxteth Park with his half brother Alois, his Irish sister in law Bridget and their son.

Europeans were colonising Liverpool before it was Liverpool; so being a European Capital of Culture is something this city is well used to. The Celts harassed the Romans, then the Saxons arrived; the Vikings turned up in 902AD and made themselves at home. Then the Normans took over; King John signed the city's first charter in 1207 and built a castle. The next foreign king to sign a charter for Liverpool was the King of Spain, Philip II (when he was married to Queen Mary) in 1556.

Liverpool has traded with Europe for ever, and Europeans came here to do business: French glass-makers in Old Swan; Italian silk manufacturers in Tithebarn Street, German sugar refiners, Portuguese wine merchants, Spanish clockmakers.

Liverpool merchants were exporting copper, iron, coal, hops, alum, soap and cloth, and importing salt fish, linen, leather and wine, back in the 1500s.

Parisian horticulturist Edouard André won the competition to design Sefton Park; it was a German, Karl Bartels, who designed the city's very icons, the Liver Birds. The Liverpool Phil has been making music with visiting Europeans, from Max Bruch and Paganini to Rachmaninov and Bartok.

Among Liverpool's twin cities around the world are Cologne and Odessa; Wirral is partner to the picturesque Transylvanian city of Sibiu, which, coincidentally, will be Capital of Culture in 2007, the year that Liverpool celebrates its 800th anniversary as a royal charter city.

When Samuel Cunard came to Liverpool more than 160 years ago from Nova Scotia to set up his transatlantic steam packet company, steel hulls, diesel turbines radar and radio were no more than science fiction

The Sefton Park Palm House is an analogy for the city's troubles: left to rot for decades by a City Council with its own agenda, it is now refurbished, brought back to life through the efforts of local entrepreneurs like Victor Greenberg.

the 30 years' war

In the 1960s Liverpool was one of the coolest cities on the planet, thanks to the amazing golden age of music, art and poetry (yes, that includes the Beatles). Ten years later the city was in the doldrums, silted up, abandoned and desperate.

After 300 years as one of the world's most powerful trading cities, with an astonishing record of innovation and enterprise. But after the war, when the May Blitz inflicted terrible damage on Liverpool, Birkenhead and Bootle, the warning signs began. Air travel took passengers and freight away from the docks; containerisation closed the south docks and put thousands of dockers out of work; corporate restructuring meant head offices moving south and big factories closing. The Toxteth riots of 1981 sounded the city's death knell, with city politics gone mad and Liverpool on the skids.

The end of the 20th century was Liverpool's worst period since the mid 1500s, when the decayed town's shrinking, plague ridden population (then fewer than 1,000) had to appeal to Queen Elizabeth I for help.

But then came Michael Heseltime, Tory 'minister for Merseyside', and the 1984 International Garden Festival. It was a momentous event, but not the end of the city's troubles, which continued to the end of the decade.

Then sanity broke out with the election of Harry Rimmer as leader of the council, and a new wave of pragmatism broke over the city council, with councillors and then local MPs waiving party political differences and working in tandem to get the city back on its feet. The Merseyside Development Corporation was dropped like a brick into the south docks, to some protest from locals, and began to restore the Albert Dock buildings – the largest group of Grade I listed buildings in the UK.

The regeneration train chugged forward, slowly gathering pace through the 1990s, with the City Challenge programme and then Objective 1 status producing over £1bn in public and private sector investment.

By the turn of the century, as Millennium celebrations were being planned, Liverpool's 30 years' war quietly ended. Thirty years of the city's nightmare became a small blip on the Millennium timeline, although for those who have lived through the dark times, it has seemed a very long haul. Liverpool and Merseyside have been reborn and now we need to see the economy thrive.

The slow growing interest and optimism of the city erupted into screams of triumph and a few sighs of relief when, in July 2003, Liverpool was named European Capital of Culture 2008. The excitement has fuelled Liverpool's renaissance and the city is almost unrecognisable from its 1980s self.

In July 2004 came more icing on the cake – after a long drawn out decision process, Liverpool's waterfront and other historic areas were declared by UNESCO to be a World Heritage Site.

Liverpool: take the up escalator!

Liverpool leads the UK in attracting inward investment. The city is a grade-A shop window that attracts the interest of investors far and wide. What a transformation from 20 and more years ago when it seemed only basement trappings were on offer.

In 2004, the city and conurbation have a vibrancy of lifestyle and commerce that competes on a European stage. Cranes dot the skyline as the renaissance continues, adding to the outstanding historic architecture of Liverpool — Britain's latest UNESCO World Heritage city.

Economically, the city region's recovery has been breathtaking: business confidence is riding high. Perhaps the greatest endorsement of the economic transformation is represented by the investment decisions of global corporations, indigenous firms and entrepreneurs to invest in the Liverpool city region. This makes it head and shoulders the most successful inward investment location in the UK in 2003/4.

So what has driven this transformation?

A marvellous mix of ingredients. Attitudes have changed. Public policymakers have reached out to the business community — creating the climate for success. Well-directed public investment, from local authorities, central government and the EU, has greatly strengthened our infrastructure. The workforce is truly a new generation with the skills and outlook to match modern commercial demands; businesses have regained that animal spirit — confidence and entrepreneurship — that characterises success.

All of these ingredients form a partnership spirit that puts business in prime position. Indeed The Mersey Partnership is an example of that — a unique alliance of over 400 businesses and public organizations across the city region of Liverpool and beyond — all pulling together to promote the competitive advantages of the region as a place to live, work, invest and visit.

Since its formation in 1993, The Mersey Partnership has supported many investors in expanding into Merseyside, creating thousands of jobs and investing millions of pounds; and we continue to welcome and support businesses considering new investments.

There is more to do as we make Liverpool a premier European city region. One thing you can be sure of is that business will be at the centre of what we do in reaching for that goal.

That's making Liverpool a place on the rise — a city where you can take the up-escalator to business success.

Mark Basnett
Head of Investment
The Mersey Partnership

entrepreneur survey

To get a snapshot of Merseyside's owner managers and their views of business in general and of corporate finance in particular, we surveyed 900 SMEs with a turnover between £0.75m and £10m.

Two of the most striking statistics were that just over half (51%) would sell their business if the right offer came along, even though 59% of the sample said their profits were up on 2003.

And not a single respondent had an independent non-exec director on their board. Not one. Some businesses had a spouse or other family member on the paperwork as a makeweight, but a working non-exec, no.

Very few – 6% – were backed by venture capital, although 39% said they were willing to explore the possibility. 70% were looking for development capital, however, and most of the amounts needed fell into the classic equity gap (£200,000 – £3m). Over a quarter said they were looking to make acquisitions.

To offer a picture of the people who responded, 43% were founders of the business, just over a quarter had bought the business and 16% inherited it. Most had two or three directors on the board, and 48% had between 11 and 50 employees.

The age of the businesses was spread fairly evenly over the last 100-odd years, with the single biggest group (15%) founded in the 1970s; 10% were less than 10 years old (of which only two were post-2000) and 7% were established in the 19th century.

Asked which important issues faced their business, the following cropped up several times:
- HR/recruitment
- interest rates
- foreign competition
- new technology
- foreign currency (euro)

and the top two pet hates are:
- insurance costs
- regulation

One respondent said the first time he tried to raise some venture capital, in 1998, his manufacturing sector 'was deemed not interesting enough'. At the second attempt in 2001 'MSIF were very supportive'.

There was the wag who, when asked to name his most important adviser, wrote: 'My Maserati dealer'. This lucky man said, when asked if would go for venture capital, said: 'Don't need capital, got loads of the stuff.' He also suggested that the government could help business by 'making it a criminal offence to be a solicitor'.

Almost every respondent said they thought that Liverpool getting the Capital of Culture title for 2008 would be a positive influence on the local economy and many said it would help their business. One comment, however, was not so positive: 'I have just returned from Hong Kong; when I arrived back in Liverpool I was disgusted and ashamed to say I am a resident of this city.' He doesn't explain why.

Why do you run your own business?

"I started my business when I became unemployed and divorced. It was a decision either to build a future or commit suicide."

What advice would you give somebody thinking about starting a business?

"Speak to as many people you can who have done the same thing, and learn from their experiences. Work on and not in the business, and focus on what really makes the business perform."

Mersey entrepreneurs

The Bibby Group is one of Liverpool's great family firms, going back six generations to John Bibby founding his shipping line in 1807. Now run by Michael Bibby, the group has three main divisions: shipping, supply chain logistics and financial services.

John Hargreaves began his rise to retail stardom on a stall at Paddy's Market. Founding the Matalan store chain in 1985, Hargreaves went on to feature in the Forbes Rich List, noted as worth over $1bn in 2003. Does this stallholder at Liverpool's farmer's market have what it takes?

If role models are needed, there are plenty of crackers along the banks of the Mersey. Across the board – from retail to manufacturing, sport to film, construction to food. Some of these thriving businesses date back 200 years or more, some are fresh on the scene.

RS Clare has been making lubricants for over 250 years, now with road markings and surface treatments too. In 1798 leading jewellers Boodle & Dunthorne was founded, and the Wainwright family have owned the business since 1880. The 19th century produced names such as Billingtons, Europe's leading importer of unrefined cane sugar – sold in 2004 to Silver Spoon after 140 of family ownership; two of the UK's leading brands of canned food – Princes and John West – are still based in Liverpool although both now subsidiaries of larger parents. A global giant – Unilever – has its beginnings on

the Wirral, where James and William Hesketh Lever (who became Lord Leverhulme) began making Sunlight Soap in 1885, and built Port Sunlight village for their workers. In 1930 Lever Brothers merged with the Dutch company Margarine Union, and Unilever was born. Now owner of massive brands from Fabergé to Bird's Eye, Persil to Pot Noodle, and Lynx to Ben & Jerry's.

In the 1920s, John Moores and two friends – one named Littlewood – founded their pools business, and opened their first store in 1932. Since then the Moores family have been a force in the city, and the business became of Europe's largest family-owned companies, with turnover of more than £2bn. The family sold out in 2002 to the Barclay Brothers.

Leonard Steinberg started his bookmaking business in Ulster in 1958 and moved to Liverpool in 1979. Now with 37 casinos and 600 betting shops in the UK, Stanley Leisure floated in 1986.

Steve Morgan, born in Garston in 1953, borrowed £5,000 from his father in 1974 and bought out his employers, Wellington Civil Engineering. He turned the business into Redrow, the housebuilders, which he floated in 1994 before cashing in £198m of shares in 2000. He still has a sizable stake in the company, as well as in a hotel group, and a small percentage of Liverpool FC.

Jon Falkingham and Tom Bloxham, founders of Urban Splash in 1993, are heading the same way, having made a major contribution to Liverpool's physical renaissance.

Some of Merseyside's leading entrepreneurs:
Martin Ainscough
Stephen Beetham
Dominic Burke
Trevor Burke
Hugh Frost
John Halewood
Asif Hamid
Peter Johnson
Colin McKeown
Lorraine Rogers
David Wade Smith
Robert Wade Smith

Rathbones, the investment fund managers, may have its corporate HQ in London these days, but its heart is in Liverpool, where the Rathbone family for many generations have exerted huge commercial, political and philanthropic influence.

World class support in the European Capital of Culture

BusinessLiverpool's role is to champion enterprise and investment and to create a world class city for business. As the gateway for business support in Liverpool, our primary objective is to create a focused and effective business support mechanism which fully meets the needs of the business community.

The core activity of BusinessLiverpool is the provision of free business support in the areas of property, finance, and workforce development — and by working in partnership with other key public and   private sector organisations to deliver a comprehensive support package that meets the needs of our clients.

Liverpool is being transformed through massive regeneration projects, but for the city to thrive and for economic growth to be sustainable long term, it needs an upsurge in business start-ups with a high rate of survival and expansion.

There is no doubt that the talent within the city is enormous, and is being fed by the constant flow of students coming to the universities and by people drawn to exciting new jobs in the city. This is a crucial time in our history and it is essential that the next generation of entre-preneurs is nurtured and inspired to establish and grow their business in Liverpool and use the city as a gateway to new global markets.

From supporting start-up businesses to expansion of local companies and securing mobile investment, BusinessLiverpool has secured more than £225m of private sector investment and has created or safeguarded more than 5,000 jobs since its launch in 2001. It is ranked as one of the top city investment agencies in the world by an independent survey and has played a key role in securing investment into Liverpool from Unisys, Bank of New York, Coutts, Bertlesman, Cains and many other companies that saw the potential for growth in our city, and are seeing that vision being achieved.

Working closely with our partner organisations — Business Link for Greater Merseyside, Liverpool Chamber of Commerce and Industry, and Liverpool City Council — ensures that BusinessLiverpool can access a wealth of information and business support to help business grow and prosper. By working closely with business and supporting entrepreneurs, we continue to make a difference to Liverpool and play a key role in its regeneration.

Christopher Baker
chairman
BusinessLiverpool

Here are 800 years of change – Liverpool's history in one frame; from the parish church of St Nicholas which dates back to the early 13th century, to the Millennium bridge across Princes Dock

With all those centuries of entrepreneurial success behind today's business community, it should be way ahead of other British cities, shouldn't it?

Perhaps it's expecting too much of a city which has been through three decades of near-collapse. Perhaps the dramatic loss of confidence both in the city and themselves has knocked the stuffing out of people who might otherwise be running businesses and creating wealth for Merseyside. Why else would this area be so far behind Manchester and Birmingham?

Perhaps Scousers are as stupid, lazy, feckless, and dishonest as they are made out to be in some quarters. Perhaps the talent and drive and courage has leached out of the gene pool and left a watered down version of history's commercial, industrial and innovative giants. Perhaps we all ought to pack up and move to Leeds.

No? Then prove it. After decades of an image so negative even the seagulls were flocking to Warrington, the world has decided that Liverpool is cool again. Maybe not yet the coolest city on the planet, but getting there.

And if London journalists and the leader of the Tory party are promoting Liverpool as a great place to be, shouldn't we start believing them?

Confidence to turn vision into reality, turn ideas into businesses, and turn small business into medium sized business – it's being pumped in with the massive private sector investment from outside the city. So breathe in the new spirit of enterprise, and get cracking.

The banks are coming back to the city. Having moved their corporate departments out of Liverpool in recent years, they have seen the sea change in the city's fortunes and they've returned. New ones have arrived, too – Coutts, for instance, is here to look after the local high net worth individuals.

The business pages of the Daily Post and Echo make good reading these days – lots of upbeat stories of businesses starting and growing, winning awards, going into new export markets, making an impact. It's inspiring stuff.

chapter 2
Making it

enterprise

'Everything we cherish about this country can only be built on the bedrock of a flourishing culture of enterprise and achievement.' – Gordon Brown, 2004

The Chancellor of Exchequer is putting some energy into the drive for a more enterprising culture in Britain; he has promised that he will cut tax and regulation for small/medium business, that he will inject a measure of enterprise into the education system, that he will work to improve the image of enterprise and break down the barriers to business.

All excellent news, and things are changing, slowly. Graduates are far more likely to want their own business, far more young people than before see business as a high status activity, and across the board people want to become their own boss rather than work for one.

But – and it's a J-Lo sized but – they don't know where to start. The biggest mental obstacle is the fear of failure; this is still a highly risk averse culture.

The single biggest barrier to setting up in business, however, is lack of access to money. A Treasury report in 2004 picked up nothing new – there's a big gap between those who want money, and those who have it to invest. Tax breaks like EIS (enterprise investment scheme) have had an impact, but it doesn't help those without the spare $10,000 to invest.

There is a vast amount of institutional money looking for good homes, but apparently few businesses they deem worth investing in. It seems that as well as an equity gap, there is a communication gap. Actually, there are several – between various segments of the business community. The North West is one of the UK's worst regions for believing that one should or could start a business. So do we organise therapy to improve self-esteem in entrepreneurs, or business skills classes?

Can you teach enterprise? Entrepreneurs are born, not made, but some of them may need their eyes opening to the possibility of using their natural talent to grow a business. Young Enterprise is a superb example of how to introduce teenagers to the world of business – kids need to know that an entrepreneur can spring from any background, regardless of age, education, gender, class, nationality, religion, or fashion sense.

Whatever information is needed can be read, bought, or found on the net; business success can come at any age, and the world is big enough to offer markets to everyone who can identify the opportunities.

On Merseyside, social enterprise is taking hold, with the number of small community businesses being started, funded and mentored to success. Unless we do something proactive to take the whole region – including the disadvantaged areas and the disaffected people – with us on the economic revival, the place will polarise and will be in danger of splitting apart again.

For once the government and the private sector are in full agreement. So let's spread the message and hold the government to its promises.

7,000 people were surveyed recently; a year later of those who said they were planning to start a business, 15% had taken action, 53% were still thinking, and 32% avoided the question.

There are 3.7m SMEs in the UK, of which some 2.5m are self-employed individuals. As a whole they produce 4% of GDP, have annual turnover of £1 trillion, and employ 12 million.

Blue collar startups account for 55% of all UK new business registrations.

the entrepreneurial personality

What is an entrepreneur? The media these days seems to equate an entrepreneur with the owner of a business, be it global.

Ask the proverbial man in the street for the name of an entrepreneur and you'll hear Branson, Bill Gates, Stelios. Locally, it might be Malcolm Walker, Steve Morgan, John Hargreaves. All well-known business figures who have built a business from scratch and made a high-profile fortune in the process.

But is every business owner an entrepreneur, and is the boardroom table the only place to find one?

No, of course not.

There are thousands of businesses run by individuals, families, and partners who only want to make a decent living and have little interest in fast growth: they would be better described as owner-managers. The business owner who claims to be an entrepreneur might have the soul of a manager and be, if not allergic, to risk, having what the doctors call an intolerance to it.

A corporate finance expert put it this way: 'Managers want rewards with no risk. After two hours in the first meeting, managers' eyes glaze over and they tend not to come back for the second meeting.'

On the other hand, inside organisations, whether it's a small company, the local authority, a FTSE 100 corporation, an orchestra or a physics lab, there are entrepreneurs: people who spot opportunities and are prepared to take a risk, work hard, make changes and push things forward. These hidden entrepreneurs might be any-where: the call centre, the shop floor, the second violins, the R&D department, even the council chamber.

It doesn't matter whether you have a PhD or left school without taking an exam; whether you come from Kensington L6 or Kensington SW1, speak Scouse or Serbo-croat. If you have a winning idea, energy, drive, are prepared to listen and learn, can find good people to join you, others to help you, and are prepared to take risks, then the rewards are there for the taking.

What about the difference between an empire builder and a serial entrepreneur? It boils down to personality. One entrepreneur might have a passion about building one company that will dominate the global market: Bill Gates and Microsoft, for instance. Another might adore new ideas and the buzz of fast growth, so creates, builds and steps back from each business as it becomes estab-lished. Richard Branson, or Stelios Hadji-Ioannou, who try very different markets: music to airlines; airlines to pizza. They are the tip of the spearhead, they are the innovators, pattern-breakers, enthusiasts for the new.

There is a difference between a true entrepreneur and an opportunist, however: an entrepreneur wants to change the world; an opportunist only wants to make a quick buck, get out and move on.

Self-awareness is key: what do you want out of life? What are your strengths? Where does your talent lie? And how can you compensate for your weaknesses?

Business holds the key to Merseyside's prosperity

Liverpool's streets are dominated by iconic buildings that testify to the city's historic wealth and trading prowess. Places such as the Cunard Building and its two neighbours at the Pier Head demonstrate the civic pride and confidence of the entrepreneurs of the day.

That same confidence, optimism and energy is needed now. Our city's past has not always been one of wealth and prosperity but over the past few years Liverpool's regeneration has been tangibly demonstrated. The city is now poised to move into its next stage of development as a Capital of Culture.

The people of Liverpool are known for their love of this city, their pride, humor and determination. For our city to prosper up to and beyond 2008 we need determination and a belief in Liverpool s future to drive that growth. We all have a part to play in growing the bedrock of Liverpool — we may not be commissioning the likes of the Cunard Building or the Albert Dock, but the business community holds the key to Merseyside's prosperity: enterprise.

Business is not just about global players such as Microsoft or Coca Cola. Business is equally about small firms in the local area. Even a small business creates wealth because it creates jobs which lead to people spending their wages here which leads to more jobs and more wealth. And small firms grown much faster, in proportion, than the giants. In turn the presence of those successful local businesses encourages not only other people to start their own companies in the area but it also helps to attract businesses from outside of the region to establish depots or offices here. Add to this the input of the local agencies who actively promote the region and you have the ingredients for sustainable growth.

Starting a business is hard and the no one would tell you otherwise but even big local names such as Matalan or Redrow were started by one entrepreneur with an idea. All it takes is that idea, the heart to take it to fruition and the courage to accept that you may not reap the rewards of your hard work immediately.

Fear of failure holds many of us back — we may be scared for example of losing the security of our regular salary, of being able to meet the mortgage. However, until you try you will never know just how successful you can be.

Antonia Potter
The Steve Stuart Partnership

starting up

Most new businesses are not looking for significant amounts of external investment – the typical start-up is funded by overdraft, redundancy money, a loan from family or friends, maybe a second mortgage, a grant or two or some prize money.

A special class of new business does attract considerable interest from venture capital providers – the so-called blue sky business, with potential for huge growth and highly attractive returns for investors. Sectors such as biotech, pharma, IT, telecoms, knowledge, and new media are high risk, but the potential rewards are high enough to attract heavyweight investors prepared to sit through the development stages.

Not only is the jargon rife in corporate finance, but it mutates faster than a supervirus, trying to keep pace with the changes in the structure and mechanism of deals. MBO, MBI, BIMBO, IBI, VIMBO, 2BO, P2P...

The basic model is the management buyout, where the management team of a company buys a controlling interest in the business from the owner, often with backing from a private equity provider. Variations on the theme include the management buy in, where an entrepreneur buys into a business, often keeping all or part of the existing management team. A BIMBO is a combination of MBO and MBI, with the existing team letting in another stakeholder manager.

VIMBO is a vendor-investing management buy-out, with part of the equity being invested by the vendor who wants the business off its balance sheet but sees a potential return from hanging on to a small stake.

The IBI, or institutional buy in, sees a venture capitalist (VC) taking the majority stake, putting its own managers into the business.

2BO is the secondary buy-out, where the VC sells its stake, usually to another VC, sometimes back to the management team. Tertiary buy-outs happen, too.

The P2P emerged in the late 1990s when the management teams of plcs, unhappy with life on the Stock Exchange, took the company off the market and back into private ownership – usually a sizable VC deal.

Then there are deals which defy such simple labels.

A deal which has proved its success is the management buy out from a parent company of a non-core division or underperforming subsidiary. It can make sense for the parent to help fund the buy-out, as it will save the inevitable redundancies resulting from a trade sale and gives the vendor control of the exit.

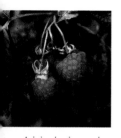

growth

If your business is growing through increasing sales, then at some stage you will have to decide how big you want to go. Is this a lifestyle business – ie one that gives you a nice living and a satisfying occupation? Or do you dream of the big time? Have you got what it takes to compete with the big boys? Are you happy for your role in the company to change (inevitable, if you go for growth)? Will you mourn the passing of the original cosy team and the hands-on way of life, or can't you wait to wave goodbye to the good old days? It's a crucial choice.

A juicy business, ripe for the plucking, is hard to resist; but is it a sweet bargain or will it taste sour?

If you decide to go for growth, there are two basic ways to grow a business: through organic growth (expanding the existing business through increased turnover and some form of development capital) or M&A (merger or acquisition, where two or more businesses are combined to advantage).

M&As are as difficult to get right as marriage, and almost as likely to fail. (Between 50% and 80% of M&A deals fail to live up to expectations.) Think of the deal as a wedding, between the courtship and married life. While you are dating, you both take care to look your best, spend lots of time with each other, want nothing more than to be together, and can't stop talking and making plans.

The wedding preparations are fraught, take months, involve an army of experts, and cost a small fortune. When the honeymoon is over, you won't spend any money, your faults show, little things irritate, and you

don't communicate.

And with rare exceptions, there is no such thing as an equal relationship – there is always a dominant partner, which usually becomes clear during the honeymoon.

No wonder mergers and acquisitions break down as often as marriages. They may not all get to the point of divorce, but if the board can't make it work well, it can be a long and frustrating relationship full of resentment, simmering discontent and occasionally vicious rows, with plans shelved and the business stagnating.

Get it right, however, and the sales turnover will jump with better profit margins after duplicated costs have been cut out, operations become more efficient, and markets can be better exploited.

The buy-and-build model became popular a few years ago, with an MBO or IBO as the platform to bolt on a series of acquisitions quickly, using private equity and debt to transform a relatively small company into a very different business. Getting the deals right and managing the acquisitions are serious challenges and not for the inexperienced or the risk-averse.

It doesn't have to be so complicated, though. A simple acquisition, of a business whose owner wants to retire, perhaps, or buying the assets of a company from the receivers, should be fairly manageable if the planning is done well and the integration managed sensitively.

Strategic thinking, and having access to funds should a good deal come up, are key to successful acquisitions.

Beware building on anything but rock solid foundations – too many companies collapse because they grow too fast.

types of money

Don't forget the Small Firms Loan Guarantee scheme – take-up rose by 40% in 2003. There are 23 lenders offering SFLG, in which the government guarantees 75% of the loans up to £250,000.

There is no shortage of money out there; the trick is to get your hands on the right kind, at the best value. If you don't have the odd million quid under your mattress that you can afford to lose, or a generous relative, you will have to pay for money to fund your business.

Except perhaps for a small and simple start-up, you will almost certainly end up with a financial pick 'n mix – some bank debt, some equity, a grant or two and perhaps a soft loan. Each comes in different shaped parcels and have their own price tags.

Grants and awards: free money in that you don't have to give them back or pay for it, but the bid process is time-consuming and you can wait ages for the money to come through.

Soft loans: Merseyside is very well served, with a number of North West based funds. There is also the UK-wide Small Firms Loan Guarantee scheme for businesses that can offer no collateral; established for some time, this has been a well proven route to cash. Soft loans may have subsidised rates of interest, capital repayment holidays, or public-sector backed guarantees that make them more attractive than commercial debt.

Found your golden goose? The eggs are valuable, but don't put them all in the one basket.

Business angels: individuals with money to invest, typically between £20,000 - £50,000 but sometimes up to £250,000 (rarely above that). They will want equity, but can make valuable contributions as non-exec directors.

Bank: not necessarily your existing bank. Talk to other high street banks, merchant banks (if the deal is

big enough), specialist lenders. Debt – whichever form it comes in – needs to be repaid and attracts interest on the loan. If the business has enough assets (intangible assets such as intellectual property are increasingly used as security for loans) then the deal may be done without giving away any equity. But lenders have less incentive to see the business succeed than an investor.

Mezzanine finance is a hybrid format between debt and equity; used most often in buy-outs and acquisitions.

Trade investors or strategic stakeholders: other companies – often customers or suppliers to the investee business – that provides some synergy and strategic gain as well as returns through royalties or an equity stake.

Venture capital: aka private equity or risk capital: expensive; entrepreneurs are polarised over its pros and cons. But it can make millionaires very fast.

Getting a customer or a supplier to take a strategic stake in your business can work brilliantly in some circumstances, with the strategic partner taking a royalty rather than equity, perhaps. There is also a major incentive for both sides to make the relationship work, and potential for valuable synergy.

How MSIF finance can benefit your business

There are all sorts of reasons why you might be thinking about looking for finance for your business, from start-up through development to retirement: but even if you don't know what type or how much finance you need, the Merseyside Special Investment Fund should be your first port of call.

MSIF is a pioneering funder providing finance for local businesses and those relocating to the region: MSIF has £80 million to invest in businesses and provides loans and equity investments of up to £3 million. Between now and 2008 MSIF aims to support around 1,000 businesses.

With every MSIF finance package come practical, money-saving support services designed to give each business the best possible chance of success. The investment teams can advise on the right kind of package for you and will look at management buy outs, buy ins, acquisitions, expansions and start-ups. Rescue situations will be considered if the business has the potential to overcome its problems and prosper.

There are now three different MSIF funds, to suit the variety of investment that a business might need.

The Small Firms Fund provides loans of up to £100,000: suitable for people starting or growing their business in almost any sector. sole traders, partnerships and limited companies can apply. Capital repayment holidays and interest rates are possible.

The MSIF Mezzanine Fund provides an important investment tool which is half way between a conventional bank loan and an equity package — which can make the difference between a transaction happening or not. It isn t a direct substitute for equity investment, but can offer investment terms often at a lower cost than an equity deal when the business has the ability to service the debt. Mezzanine finance is typically used to back more established propositions rather than start ups.

The Venture Fund is MSIF's largest fund containing £40 million. It provides equity investments in return for a minority stake in the business — often to companies with strong growth potential, where funding to develop the business is either not available or appropriate through conventional bank lending.

MSIF's equity investments are designed to allow businesses to grow faster and more efficiently.

Mark Fuller
Merseyside Special Investment
Fund

the equity gap

In 2003 VCs invested £263m in 427 UK start-up and early stage companies (up 7% from 2002). Investment in the technology sector rose by 50% to £817m.

Path blocked? There are so many routes to funding that with good advice a strong proposition will always find another doorway.

Although the UK has Europe's largest private equity industry, its focus is on larger and larger deals; in the mid 1990s a £20 million deal in the North West was big news; now it is chicken feed, with VCs looking at billion pound investments in global businesses.

For the vast majority of business owners, the amount of money they need is often too small to interest the institutional investors. They may be able to raise up to a quarter of a million quid from various sources (family, friends, bank etc), but a business looking for anything between £250,000 and £2m will fall into the equity gap.

There are various reasons for VCs being unwilling to look at small investments – one of the biggest is that the cost of doing deals is disproportionate. It doesn't cost 500 times more to do a billion pound deal than a £2m deal, in other words. Nursing a relatively small business through the deal, let alone the first three years of the relationship, can be hugely time-consuming, with a relatively small return at the end of it all. Small companies also less likely to have experienced management teams in place and are a higher risk for the VC.

For the company looking for cash, the costs of a small VC deal are high, demand a lot of management time and maybe a big change in company culture; they will certainly put pressure on the business to outperform their targets – all of which may be too high a price to pay.

But there are options, even within the venture capital industry, and Merseyside is well served.

sources of equity: business angels

Business angels – wealthy individuals who invest in growing businesses – come in all sorts of guises and can be found from many sources.

The classic angel has probably sold a business or taken early retirement from a board position, and want to invest where they can have some management involvement and get some fun out of it as well as high capital growth. (Angels can get tax relief through the Enterprise Investment Scheme.)

Angels can give their businesses enormous amounts of valuable advice, contacts, and hands-on help. If they are successful entrepreneurs, they will understand the nature of risk and can be brilliant mentors. But they can also be quirky, controlling, and difficult, so it's vital that the cash comes with the right personality to fit with your business and your team. Take references.

They can make decisions quickly, going on gut instinct rather than formal due diligence, and they can choose investments on grounds which have little to do with market sentiment – the choice could be fuelled by moral values, social preferences, even childhood dreams; emotion and whim could be as strong as marketing or financial drivers. Many angels are prepared for a longer term investment than the average institution, with an exit in five years or so, rather than three.

Some venture capital deals hinge on the commitment of a fairly small fraction of the total from a business angel – their confidence in you can make the difference.

To find a business angel you can use formal networks, like TechInvest, a well-established public sector agency in the North West; it runs seminars and events to bring angels and businesses together. There are numerous national databases and networks in the UK – a quick search on the net will bring up half a dozen. Get into the informal networks through your advisers, who will all have contacts looking for possible investments.

Watch out for the terms of the deal: and beware the whims of an angel who wants control.

Merseyside is well served with access to venture capital funds for SMEs, particularly for deals that fall into the equity gap. The North West Equity Fund (deals up to £0.5m), the Rising Stars Growth Fund, the UK High Tech Fund and most important for the local economy, the pioneering Merseyside Special Investment Fund (MSIF), now the model for regional funds around the UK. Set up in 1996, in its first five years MSIF invested £32m in nearly 700 SMEs; with EU Objective One backing, MSIF can take bigger risks than commercial lenders. Venture Fund investments are anything from £150,000 to £3m.

For larger deals, of £3m and above, there is a list of VCs with a track record in the region. In 2004 Lloyds TSB Development Capital (LDC) opened an office in the city – evidence of their faith in Liverpool's return to an enterprise culture. The doyen of VCs, 3i, had an office in Liverpool until 2002; now the nearest is in Manchester.

Along with 3i in Manchester there is Altium Capital, Aberdeen Murray Johnstone, ECI, Montagu, Granville, Isis, Barclays Private Equity and Barclays Ventures, HSBC Private Equity. National names, for the big deals and blue sky investments, include Alchemy, Close Brothers, Candover, Legal & General Ventures, Gresham, CVC, and many others.

But there is little point in approaching VCs directly – better by far to go through an adviser with a track record in getting deals away. A savvy corporate finance specialist can save you time, money and heartache.

Access to the new £26.7m Liverpool Seed Fund comes through Liverpool Ventures, an incubator set up to generate deal flow and give post-investment support and business management, from a network of mentors and non-execs.

Venture capital trusts (VCTs) were launched in 1995 to encourage individual investors to put money into SMES; the protection of a fund manager and attractive tax breaks offset the higher risk of unquoted companies. By 2001 VCTs had raised £1bn for SMEs.

debt and asset finance

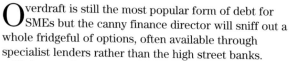

Underfinancing a deal can blight it from the start: it's one of the commonest mistakes made in business. But don't let lenders talk you into taking on more than you can chew, either

Overdraft is still the most popular form of debt for SMEs but the canny finance director will sniff out a whole fridgeful of options, often available through specialist lenders rather than the high street banks.

High street banks and merchant banks have regional acquisition finance or development capital teams. But as the money markets evolve, new products are constantly being invented, or imported from the USA, where innovative lending has been way ahead of the UK.

Talk to other banks and specialist lenders and look hard at fees and the small print, and negotiate.

Independents can win deals from the high street banks by offering better leverage, whether against trade debtors, stock, machinery, property or the order book.

Competition is fierce, so make sure that your lenders are flexible enough to cope if cashflow isn't steady from month to month. If the business is seasonal, or if you have to react fast to profitable opportunities, talk to a specialist short-term lender, who can invent a specific solution for each situation rather than offering only a standard range of financial products.

One of the fastest growing forms of lending for SMEs is factoring and invoice discounting (or receivables finance). This has had to recover from a negative image as the lending of last resort: having a factor was a sign of a failing company. No more: factoring is increasingly popular with SMEs and banks will often urge their SME clients with overdrafts to talk to the bank's factoring offshoot. Thinking of eggs in baskets, however, it is worth shopping around; talk to the independents, particularly those with a strong local base.

Receivables finance, in a nutshell, is reliable cashflow. For a company in an industry where credit terms are 60, 90 or even 120 days, and late payment is rife, this form of finance smoothes out cashflow glitches and protects a fast-growing business from the classic cashflow trap, where orders can't be fulfilled fast enough. Plenty of businesses go spectacularly bust despite a brilliant sales team and a bursting order book, because customers aren't paying their bills in time and there's no cash in the bank to get the work churned out.

How it works: as you issue each invoice to customers, you get an immediate percentage from the factor (up to 80-90%, depending on industry sector and other variables), and the balance when the customer pays up.

With invoice discounting, you handle your own sales ledger and credit control; the customer is not aware you are using receivables finance. A factor, on the other hand, will take over the whole credit control process, from checking out new customers, the administration of your sales ledger, issuing invoices and debt recovery. Your customers know that you have outsourced to a factor, and therefore credit control is going to be strict.

You pay interest on the amount borrowed, and the factor also takes a 'small percentage' of the invoice value. Shop around for competitive fees and interest.

Banks are less fond of overdrafts since a 2001 case in New Zealand threatened banks' security over clients' assets. Ask your bank manager to explain the Brumark case and its implications to you

Receivables finance has its downsides: factors offer varying percentages of credit to different industry sectors. Some will offer credit limits of, say, £7,000 per job rather than a % of invoices.

Check how aggressive your factor's debt recovery process is: you don't want to lose your customers' goodwill

Unlocking the value in Merseyside's business assets

Raising finance presents an increasingly complex challenge for SMEs, made even more difficult by the plethora of funding bodies and advisers. Research studies consistently identify cash flow constraints as the biggest problem facing UK owners and managers, with three out of five firms resorting to bank debt and almost a quarter falling back on their personal savings. Fewer than 20% of respondent SMEs consider alternative asset based lending options.

Unlocking the value of assets via factoring or invoice discounting, instantly accelerating cash flow, can enable the entrepreneur to expand his business. Trade finance facilities can also finance future transactions by funding stock purchases to satisfy confirmed orders.

Findings indicate that local utilisation of non-traditional sources of working capital funding remains at lower levels on Merseyside than elsewhere.

It is now largely acknowledged that the vilified Merseyside grant culture — tranches of non-repayable funding advanced to marginal or non-viable businesses — is a thing of the past. Issues today relate to a lack of awareness of the options available for local SMEs. But the concern remains that an unconscious insularity remains on Merseyside.

How far this state of affairs can be attributed to social, historical or economic factors is unclear. Certainly, the awareness of working capital options among professional advisers and their entrepreneurial clients could be enhanced. Merseyside SMEs need to be more stringent with their stated funding requirements adequately supported by appropriate financial information and business planning.

Could a perceived reluctance to use professional advisers be reflected in the continuing withdrawal from Liverpool of the corporate finance arms of the major accountancy firms? The Merseyside SME profile may be problematic in this respect. Local conditions would appear to exacerbate the problems facing businesses progressing from start up to stability and on to steady growth.

All parties acknowledge the need to pump prime the SMEs in the local economy and yet there remains a dearth of local providers of alternative forms of working capital. Merseyside entrepreneurs and advisers would do well face up to the challenge of understanding and being receptive to alternative methods of unlocking unexploited value in their assets before funders are tempted to throw away the key.

David Hinder
Bibby Factors (NW) Ltd

Venture capitalists are not universally loved. Like Liverpool, they suffer from a negative image in some quarters. Business owners or former business owners – may call them vulture capitalists, or 'those greedy bastards'. Others may paint them as pantomime villains and hiss whenever they are mentioned. One business guru says, to every audience, that there is only one source of money worse than VCs, 'and that's the mafia. Except that at least you know where you are with the mafia.'

Harsh words. And of course, in some cases, justified. Not every deal is signed; not every investment makes money, and the VCs play a part so must take a share of the blame. Some individuals within VC houses are more talented, competent, ethical or committed than others.

The same could be said of SMEs and their owners. Ask the VCs. Not to mention bankers, lawyers, estate agents and journalists.

On the other hand: each year private equity firms invest several billion pounds in about 1,200 growing UK businesses. Over 80% of VC backed companies say they wouldn't have existed at all, or would have grown more slowly without VC investment. Over 75% feel that their private equity investors had made a major contribution as well as providing money.

Beyond general prejudice, there are common misunderstandings, such as:

– venture capitalists take a majority shareholding: well, no, not always. The VCs want enough of a stake to make the deal worthwhile, but they want the management team to have the incentive to perform. The VC will build in safeguards such as the ability to get rid of poor managers. The percentage stake is not the most important figure in the deal – it's what happens at exit.

– VCs want control of the business: why would they? If they could run the business, presumably they'd be running one like it. Day to day operations are the management's job; the VC will want to keep an eye on strategic decisions and the non-exec they appoint will have influence on the board. Where the VC will exercise control is if it all starts to go wrong.

– VCs are only in it for the money. Well, yes, that's their business, to make good returns for their investors. But a VC is backing the management team, without whom they can't make a bean. If the management team wins, the VC wins. Everybody happy.

VCs can get it wrong. The dotcom bubble in the late 1990s proved that, when everyone seem to forget the fundamentals and indulge in mass fantasy. But VCs are only human; they're under pressure to perform every bit as much as the management teams they back.

The trick, of course, is to know all the downsides and early in the game ask them awkward questions; and if the personal chemistry is wrong, follow your instincts. Business is about people first, money second. If you don't like and trust the people you're committed to, the chance of success is not so much slim as anorexic.

VC backed companies outperform leading UK business. Over a five year period, on average, VC backed business showed annual increases of:
- *sales by 21%*
- *exports by 11%*
- *investment by 21%*
- *jobs by 19%*

To talk of venture capital as a single concept isn't really fair; there are huge differences between a £50m buyout from a plc, an injection of £5m development capital into an SME, and a £1m bet on an early-stage biotech business. The objectives, speed and culture of each is very different. We need new definitions.

There's nothing quite like
the feel of cool, crisp cash

What do management teams expect when they start the MBO trail? Is it really possible to trouser a million quid at the end of three years if you don't have a pile of cash to put into the business? Apart from the Lottery and winning Pop Idol, there are few quicker ways to make a fortune and stay out of jail.

This is crudely how it works. Two managers buy out a company for £1.4m; the managers put in £50,000 each, the bank puts in £300,000 and the VC puts in £1m.

The VC wants an internal rate of return (IRR) of 30% and an exit after three years, by which time they reckon the company will be worth £5m. On that IRR, the VC's stake 'grows' each year by a compound 30%, so in Yr 1 it is £1m; in Yr 2 it is £1.3m, in Yr 3 it is £1.69m, and at the end of Yr 3 it is £2.2m. That is 44% of the company's £5m value. So although the VC has put in far more cash than the management, they take a 44% stake, leaving the managers with 56% of the business.

So if, after three years, they sell the business for £6m, slightly more than estimated, the VC will get £2.64m, and the managers will walk away with £1.68m each.

Dividing the equity pie is not necessarily down to personal wealth, either. VCs look to buy-out candidates to put up enough of their own cash to motivate them, but the stake is also based on non-financial contributions, recognising leadership, for instance, or IP ownership. The man with the million-pound brain may be worth at least the same stake as the one with all the cash.

After the buy-out of the camping equipment chain Milletts, every £100,000 invested by the management team turned into about £40 million at exit. No chickenfeed.

NB: IRRs are a bit old hat. These days it's more about cash multiples – eg two or three times what was invested.

Entrepreneurs can find the deal process
something of an arcane ritual

When it comes to doing a deal for the first time, many entrepreneurs are horrified by the frustration and stress of the last-minute negotiations, the petty-fogging detail, the late nights, the hanging around and the staggering amounts of paper. It's an emotional rollercoaster, and you need a strong arm to lean on – find the right adviser.

There are always areas of conflict, with your fellow directors and your team, let alone the other side. There are endless details to be thrashed out, all of which have ramifications that need to be thought through.

Whoever you are dealing with – vendor or buyer – might go back on terms agreed, or indeed change their minds altogether and pull the deal. The trainee solicitor could split up with his girlfriend and lose concentration for long enough to leave out a crucial word in an expensive clause, not spotted till an hour before completion.

You sit around for hours, if not days, waiting for phone calls to confirm terms. For some reason, completion tends to happen in the wee small hours after a gruelling paper-strewn marathon with black coffee and cold pizza to keep you going.

You are so consumed by the deal process that you lose touch with what's going on in the office and find chaos and lost orders when you eventually get back to normal post-deal life, which causes havoc with your precious cash flow forecasts and performance targets.

But at the end of it, you have a sparkling future and the promise of untold rewards fizzing in your veins.

'The completion meeting took 26 hours; it was our lawyers' Christmas party that evening, and the poor secretary was working all night. But we did at least have our turkey dinners brought in.'

'The negotiations on this one deal were dragging on over a sensitive price issue. About five months in to the process, the entire team we were dealing with at the VC upped and left for another firm in London. So the VC pulled out of our deal and we had to start all over again. I tell you, I could have murdered them.'

contracts and warranties

Even with covenants on monthly performance targets, having a good relationship with your investors could mean that a bad three months following a good half-year could be smoothed over

There's no point in escaping from the prison of employment, to shackle yourself to your own business with heavy duty warranties and agreements

The paperwork can be the doom of a deal – or rather what's in the documents. Killer clauses include the terms on which directors leave, warranties, performance bonuses, and voting rights. Many a deal has foundered because these issues are not tackled early enough.

Every deal starts with a standard investment agreement, shareholders' agreement and contracts of employment; but negotiations over what gets added, amended or erased can be tortuous. This is one area where good advisers earn their fees many times over; they will know what the investors will budge on, and what is written in stone.

Warranties, which give the investor some protection if the entrepreneur screws up, can hurt: they're meant to. The level is set high enough to make you think very hard about how much you believe in your business, and how committed you are to making it work; investors look at your personal assets before setting warranties.

In the contract, look very closely at the good leaver / bad leaver clauses. These are what will determine what happens if you leave the company, and depend hugely on whether you leave on good terms or bad, and how far into the life of the investment. If you get fired for gross misconduct after six months, you will get less than if you perform brilliantly for two years then get ill and have to quit. Percentages, definitions of performance, valuation, timescales: all play a vital part in how much you end up with, so take very good advice.

personal and family life

Personal and family life is a major consideration for an ambitious business owner. Whether or not family members are involved in the business, home and business life can have serious effects on each other and must be factored into the equation when planning to buy or grow a business. Ask any divorce lawyer.

Doing the deal is a stressful process that takes a physical and emotional toll. And once the deal is done the late nights and working weekends don't end.

Is your family 100% behind your business dreams? Giving up a good salary plus perks for an uncertain future may be too much to ask. Failure could mean the house, all the trappings, even the social life have to go.

Going into business with your spouse is another story: it can be hugely exciting and successful, but there must be safety valves built into the relationship at both ends. Needs clear thinking and a lot of discussion.

Major considerations are pensions and tax: two of the most mind-numbingly complex areas of finance. But unless planned well they can have disastrous effects on the future.

Take very good advice on protecting shares and control in changing personal circumstances, eg second marriages and the like.

Can your family weather the storms?

family business

The family business is the backbone of the UK private sector, with over 40% of firms with a turnover between £5m and £100m in private hands. This is a prime market for the corporate finance community and offers huge opportunity for swift and steady growth.

But corporate finance specialists are frustrated at all the good family businesses that are just dogging along, happy with the status quo. 'They won't contemplate private equity because they perceive VCs as too aggressive, and they fear losing control,' is a typical comment. And almost by definition there is an inherent culture clash. 'A traditional, debt-averse third generation family business is not going to find private equity attractive – not least because they don't want some outsider foisted on to their board telling them what to do. Their great-grandfather started the firm when God was a lad, after all.'

Some VCs have little time for the family business, claiming the owner-managers have little ambition, no clear leadership and the prospect of a family feud always around the corner.

However, one of the danger points for every family business is when one generation hands over to the next. Succession can be an issue that rips the family to shreds, not to mention the business; this is where bringing in an external equity provider can turn up trumps.

Say that of two brothers running a business, one wants to sell up and swan off to Magaluf with his new wife and half the proceeds – while the other still has

ambitions for the business and won't hear of selling. Or say that a woman has inherited a business from her father and wants to build the business to hand on to her daughter, but wants to boost the management team and kick the business into serious growth. In both cases, given the underlying strength of the business, finding the right VC to inject both capital and management could multiply the companies' worth while keeping the family in the frame. There's nothing to stop the family buying the VC out at exit, of course, if they have the cash.

Having a VC on board, with the discipline of working with an external investor and the pressure to meet targets, can transform a family business and create real value for the next generation.

living with investors

At the first meeting, everyone is all smiles. But beware of Cheshire Cats – as Alice discovered, it is extremely frustrating when everything vanishes except for the smile.

Be realistic – set achievable targets. Never promise what you aren't sure you can deliver. Over-performing is better.

A clue to the reality of life with external investors:
• venture capital is known as risk capital for a reason.

Of every ten VC-funded businesses, three will go bust, three will stagnate, three will do OK, and one will make a fortune. Pretty much the same formula applies to many areas of our lives, so to pretend that getting VC backing guarantees your success is naive in the extreme.

Often managers don't fully appreciate what they're getting into; they think that once they've bought the business and got rid of the vendor, they're away. They don't realise that the investing institution is, in effect, the new boss and that they are hedged about with restrictive covenants, drag-along clauses, swamping rights and the rest. Hence the need for top notch advice and meticulous research and preparation.

Management have every opportunity to wreck the business after the deal is done; the VC can make mistakes before deal completion that puts the venture under unbearable strain from the start. But despite the high attrition rate, some say that if they didn't have some failures they weren't being aggressive enough in the search for potential star investments.

Being too aggressive and going for a deal even at too high a price will hand the management team a poisoned chalice – they have to try to make the deal work but they will struggle to meet targets if the numbers are wrong at the start.

A majority shareholding won't help, either. In the

agreement will be a share structure that gives the VC powers that override the management team in certain situations – which is how the chief executive can find himself sitting on the pavement surrounded by his belongings with a pay-off cheque in his fist. It happens.

On the other hand, the arrival of a VC in the life of a business can free up the management to manage, giving them enthusiastic backing and the confidence to push the business forward. 'Having access to that weight of institutional money, and having investors on board who believed in us was a fantastic boost,' said one newly liberated entrepreneur. 'Our advisers had made sure we got good terms at the start, and once the details were out of the way we were cheered on our way. Board meetings are constructive and productive, and we couldn't be more delighted with the way things have worked out.'

If your contact at the VC gets another job and leaves, there is a danger that the replacement is not so supportive, or that you just don't get on. Get your advisers on the case – don't let the business suffer because you're too polite to say anything.

If the board meeting is one long fencing match, then something needs mending. It could be a bad choice of non-exec, or it could be one or more of the management team causing trouble. Lively debate is one thing; petty squabbling and little vendettas are quite another.

Get the deal right, and if it's not right, don't sign

Bringing private equity investment into a business is usually a once in a lifetime event that may be the key decision that defines the personal rewards of the hard work demanded in developing their business.

The transaction is a complex one involving due diligence, business planning, negotiation of terms, warranties, and the introduction of at least one non-exec to the board. The entrepreneur has to assume at least some of the trappings of an employee, answerable to his board of directors and shareholders.

For a team, let alone an individual, it can seem daunting and all-consuming just to get through it, let alone secure as commercially advantageous a deal as possible.

Of course I would say this, wouldn't I, but in this type of intense commercial environment it is essential to have an advisory team you can rely on and work with, and from whose commercial know-how you can draw strength and confidence. In choosing a team (at least a corporate finance accountant and lawyer) go for experience, independence, compatability and pragmatism. Ask for recommendations from people who have done successful deals, and get references

Experience: this is a key event in your life. Choose advisers who have been around the block and know the ground rules. They should be able to manage the process bringing you in only for key decisions along the way. Obviously, the less time you are taken away from running the business, the better.

Independence: an entrepreneur invests so much in the process that there can be a mentality of doing the deal at all costs. Pick an advisor who is not afraid to draw a line in the sand on key issues. Bear this in mind when agreeing fee structures that solely links fees to success, when success is defined as signing the deal. This puts pressure on everyone to agree a deal at any costs when the best advice would be not to go ahead.

Compatibility: it makes sense to work with someone you like and can get on with; remember that as the deal rolls on you will see more and more of your advisers.

Pragmatism: your advisers ability to understand commercial realities and constraints and focus on the key areas will ultimately get the deal done, and maybe even keep the fees down.

Philip Whitehurst
DWF

get the best out of your advisers

In the village of the North West professional and financial community, having advisers who know the other advisory teams could mean the difference between success and failure for the deal. It's vital to pick a team with excellent contacts and a track record. Shop around, ask successful entrepreneurs for their recommendations.

Advisers are always crucial, but never more than in corporate finance. Bad advice can be disastrously expensive; good advice can make millions for entrepreneurs.

The first task for a lead adviser is to do themselves out of a deal if it's not feasible. If they're so desperate for fees that they'll press on with a dud deal – or are too cowardly to be honest with you, you don't want them.

Then you need to field your team – lawyers, bankers, angels, etc. Look for a track record, ask around.

You want advisers with hard noses, commercial heads, broad shoulders and sometimes brass necks. Odd-looking they may be, but they will lead you through the tortuous and exhausting deal process to completion, and if you're any good at your job of growing the busines, you can test them next time with a 2BO or an IPO. If your adviser takes pleasure in blinding you with jargon, of course, you are allowed to shoot them.

Are you on target? Let your advisers make sure you're properly primed and sighted

Non-executive directors are there to look after share-holders' rights and to make sure the investment is being looked after. Investors will want a seat on the board, and may also insist on a non-exec to fill a vital gap in the management's expertise.

How they are rewarded is down to negotiation. Some will want a set annual fee. Others, if they are convinced of the company's potential, may accept a small equity stake and waive their fee. Some want both.

What makes a good non-exec? It is not only their con-tacts or their industry knowledge that is of primary importance, but their independence – they must be able to resist an aggressive CEO and challenge the board. One of their favourite words is 'why?'. Technical man-agers can try to bamboozle the board with jargon; the non-exec should ask questions until it is crystal-clear.

Successful entrepreneurs are not always good non-execs, who should have a cool head, the ability to see over the top of the trees, a good grasp of those tiresome regulatory issues, skill in soothing fevered brows and an ego that doesn't need to make itself felt.

One popular non-exec remembered his first board appointment: 'I said not a word for three meetings, just listened and absorbed until I got to know the other board members and the business.'

The worth to an ambitious business of a really good non-exec is beyond rubies, but they can be harder to find than a black pearl in a slag heap.

Look for names which crop up time and again to find the really good non-execs. But beware: some will be popular because they turn up, eat the biscuits, and cause no strife. Non-execs should be stirring up your board, not just stirring sugar into their coffee.

A non-exec with half a brain will apply due diligence before accepting a seat on any board – they will, after all, be fully liable for board decisions and could end up in the prison cell next to the real rogue director if the business goes pear shaped.

exit

It is essential that owner managers going into a deal with a private equity provider builds terms for their exit into the deal from the start. It is equally essential to sort out tax implications before the deal. If there are ratchets built into the buy out deal, with shifts in value with each bolt-on, for instance, the Inland Revenue will have something to say about it. Ask.

You will have to exit your business at some time, even if it's feet first in a box. Retirement, handing over to your kids, selling to the management team or another business, floating the company, or going bust. They're all ways to get out, and the fewer the shareholders, the less pressure to exit. A family row, however, can create enormous pressure to sell up and divide the proceeds.

If you have external investors, they will have built an exit strategy into the deal from the start. VCs usually want an exit after three years, although this can change, with VCs putting in round after round of funding over a decade or more, if the company is growing sales and margins and it suits the VC's investment policy.

The main exit routes are: trade sale, sale to a financial institution, flotation or, at worst, liquidation. The preferred route at the outset may not prove desirable when it comes to it, particularly if the company has not come up to scratch and the VC wants out whether or not the management team agree. Think it through first.

Floating your company is the most glamorous way to go, or it used to be. A listing on the Stock Exchange proved the business had arrived. Now the various markets, from the LSE and AIM to OFEX in the UK, and the likes of NASDAQ in the US, are just mechanisms to choose from when it comes to moving the business to the next stage.

Lots of companies that would have gone for a listing now prefer to go for venture capital, preferring to report to one investor rather than a roomful of them.

If flotation is right for the business, the first choice is which market to go for. The Official List or AIM? Or is OFEX all you need? Things to think about: the varying costs of each route, how much scrutiny the company will have to bear, how easy the shares will be to trade (liquidity), how much money you want to raise, how often you will want to go back for further fundraising later, how much investment can you make in wooing analysts and upping the companys' profile, how much management time you will have to devote to admin and investor relations... and so on.

A big warning sign: the Stock Market is notoriously fickle and fashion-driven, and unfeasibly short-termist, looking for quick capital gain and strong performance. A depressed share price can put severe curbs on company growth, and share price often has little to do with normal performance measurements such as sales growth or profitability. But if you get it right, there's nothing like it – companies can grow fast and make a lot of money.

Launched in 1995, AIM – the Alternative Investment Market – was greeted with enthusiasm, but its first five years saw some early scandals and a sharp drop in popularity. But teething troubles dealt with, AIM is now a successful part of the corporate finance landscape. It was designed to be easier, quicker and cheaper to float on AIM than on the main market, but in practice the cost of due diligence and preparation is not far off costs for a full listing. Once on AIM, though, regulation is not so onerous and it is good practice for a full listing later.

In some ways, the Stock Market has some profound differences to other capital infrastructures, and entrepreneurs need to do some serious research and rack up hefty fees getting hard-nosed advice before deciding.

The flotation process and the preparation for it takes months, even years, and can be a terrible distraction for management. Not to mention exhausting.

The potential volatility of share prices, which can have more to do with front page news than company performance, can make it hard for the management to plan for the mid to long term.

In other words, make abslutely sure that flotation is right for your company before you commit to it.

The success of a trade sale depends on various factors, not least is the company's performance and future potential.

An early question will be to find out whether the individuals selling the business are dispensable: will the business survive without its head? Vendors may be tied in to a fixed contract or an earn-out over anything from six months to five years. The buyer may insist that the vendor work hard for his pile of cash; for that matter, the vendor might want to keep running the business simply because he enjoys it.

If you are selling, can you find out why the buyer wants your business – is it to strip out the assets and dump everything else, or will life go on much as before? It would be a stony-hearted entrepreneur who didn't have concerns for his employees, suppliers and customers. Different buyers see different assets; your competitors will have a different agenda to a buyer somewhere along your supply chain.

But if you are approached by someone waving a big wad of cash, it must be tempting to grab it and run.

Think, though, about announcing the news to your workforce. You may think you're up for it, but entrepreneurs have found the reality to be something like a bereavement, with guilt and regret swamping the pleasure of putting all the money in the bank.

It will all depend on the buyer's plans – if he has been candid with you and isn't planning to asset strip.

If you need to search for a trade buyer, there are business brokers who will help, for an upfront fee plus up to 10% of the sale price.

Before you offer up your business for sale, the books must be in good order, obviously, and all the regulatory paperwork up to date.

Advice from those who have done it: Carry on running the business as normal until the day the money is in your bank account. Decide early on what price you want and don't compromise. Get out while the going is good.

The secondary buy-out is often where the
business really takes off

If you are close to exit from a venture capital backed deal, and assuming your VC is not trying to offload your business because it has been rubbish, a secondary buy-out can be the time when the business really takes off.

How attractive the deal is to you will depend on how well the business has performed – if you have exceeded expectations, you could well be in the driving seat for this next deal; if you have failed to meet targets, the VC will be driving the sale.

There is no fixed shape to a secondary buy-out. Typically, the existing venture capital provider realises their share of the business by selling to another VC, leaving the management team in place and the business to carry on largely as before – although the new investor will doubtless want to make some changes.

But almost anything is possible; the VC might sell everything back to the original owner, or the VC and the original owner might sell to the management team.

If the business has not done well for the VC, it is more likely to go to a trade sale; what VC would contemplate buying out a dud investment by another VC?

The popularity of 2BOs has grown – 2004 was a record year for 2BO deals in the UK – they have become the favorite alternative to a flotation.

Tertiary buyouts and whatever the term is for a series of four are also increasingly getting done as VCs look for more creative ways to add value and return value to their investors.

If you have no external investors in your business already, sale to a financial institution could be an efficient choice of exit.

Twelve of the 43 deals completed in Q3 of 2004 were secondary buyouts. They accounted for 54% of the quarter's value, and dominate the quarter's value tables – eight of the top ten deals by value were 2BOs. These secondary deals introduced a healthy degree of liquidity to the private equity market last year.

Don't build on sand. When you come to write the proposal, remember: what any financier wants to see, however visionary the idea, is that the vision is anchored in bedrock. One of the most galling lessons of the dotcom bubble, when the 'old economy' model was chucked out of the pram, was that however radical the new technology, business fundamentals don't really change.

Cash is king. Watch the costs. Don't sacrifice margins for turnover. Collect money you are owed. Talk to your bank. Don't overstock. Keep your customers happy. Underpromise and overdeliver. Have a clear strategy. Know your market. Seek good advice and act on it. Pay your bills. Look after your employees. Don't put all your eggs in one basket. Watch the costs. Cash is king.

If you can't exhibit the most beautiful of models (no overheads, low cost of sales, cash up front, big margins, pent-up demand etc) then work hard to eliminate as many flaws as possible.

Be inventive and innovative – not just with the product but as importantly with the process. Benchmark your operation against the best, and never stop improving. Be consistent. Lead by example. Use your employees' brains as well as their hands. Think green – cut out waste. Give something back to the community.

Easier by far to build the model from scratch – trying to change the culture of an existing business is tough, and takes time. But a beautiful model attracts attention and investment, so become a business sculptor.

Beware of boom industries. If you're going to exploit a short lived fad, then do it fast and get out. Technology evolves and develops with dizzying speed: can you afford to keep up?

The true value of a business is what someone is prepared to pay for it.

One way to estimate the value of a target business is to count the cash in the bank and look at the confirmed orders for the next six months. Ignore the potential of intellectual property; if it proves valuable, then it's a great bonus.

business plans

Before the VC does its due diligence on your business, do your due diligence on the VC. Look at their figures; talk to their investees, ask around. It's a small world, and the corporate finance world loves to gossip. Start drinking in the pubs round Castle Street and go to professional networking events. Read the business magazines, specially the gossip pages. Spend some time on the net reading up on deals. Sniff out the individuals with talent. Ask questions ad nauseam. Research, research, research. Get advice. Ask more questions. Check the answers.

No business plan, no money. And what investors and lenders are looking for is not a tatty old sheaf of Excel spreadsheets and some back-of-fag-packet waffle.

Ancient structures survive when they are built on classical principles. Elegance, strength, and beauty.

VCs want to see a solid business. They want to see good cash flows. They want to see a good management team in place. People, cash, structure, vision.

Other questions VCs will ask:
- Has the team worked together before?
- Does the team have relevant experience?
- Has the team agreed on a common goal?
- Do the founders know their weaknesses?
- Are they ready to correct them?
- Are the founders clear about their future roles?
- Is the ownership of the company clear?
- What is the worst case scenario?

Whoever is reading the business plan will want to see hard evidence that a market exists and access is open. If the business exploits intellectual property, how well is it protected? Does the company have its systems and processes sorted out and working smoothly?

Where does the revenue come from? How many income streams are there? How realistic are the cash flow forecasts? What evidence is there to back up assumptions and forecasts? Is there a stringent SWOT analysis? How sensitive is the business plan? Has it been tested? Are you asking for enough money?

The discipline of working up a good business plan is valuable in itself. It will force you to examine your business and yourselves. Shining a metaphorical light into shadowy corners can turn up surprises, not always pleasant ones at that. It shows up the gaps in expertise and where resources are needed.

A business plan is a dry run – even if it is, effectively, guesswork when it comes to forecasts – where you can test your idea to destruction, in risk-free theory.

Get your advisers to pull the business plan to pieces and challenge every aspect of it. That process will stand you in excellent stead for the presentation to potential investors and lenders.

A big weakness of the venture capital industry is that a lot of good businesses are ignored because they don't fit the current fashion for what is deemed sexy. But if the fundamentals are strong enough, the sector becomes much less of a priority.

The usual response from harassed owner managers, when they are urged to spend some time on strategy, is brief and Anglo-Saxon. Pressures of daily business life are relentless without finding space for a benchmarking initiative or time for a time management course. And as for taking time away from HQ to contemplate the corporate navel and think up a more sophisticated strategy than merely keeping the bank at bay...

But one of the things that finance providers love to see is evidence of strategic thinking, and a well researched plan that is regularly revised and updated.

Financiers assessing business plans will look for the Holy Grail of blue sky potential built on a rock solid model. So strategy and marketing – in its old fashioined sense of analysing the market to find the exploitable gaps in it – will not only win brownie points from the financiers but put you ahead of most businesses, whose owners and managers are busy trying to catch up.

The River Mersey has always attracted risk-takers and innovators, not to mention its fair share of explorers, who risked their lives, not just their houses, on the chance of fortune and, sometimes, fame.

With any proposal that heads into new territory, the financier will look for torch, whistle, ropes and helmets, first aid kit and a very detailed map – and would love it if there were belt and braces too, just for good measure. An expert on board to lead the way is best, but at the very least take clear instructions and a satellite phone.

"Planning is an unnatural process; it is much more fun to do something. The nicest thing about not planning is that failure comes as a complete surprise, rather than being preceded by a period of worry and depression."

Sir John Harvey-Jones

"Failure is a great teacher. We try and hire people who have suffered failure and understand that mistakes in core structure, forecast or competitiveness are serious problems."

Bill Gates

However slick the business plan might be, it needs to be reflected in the day to day operations. Like incompetence, fraud can be difficult to hide when the prospective investor steps through the company's front door. One VC relates: 'My favourite fraud was a high end jewellery business. We discovered that the reason the CEO couldn't get the inventory down was because he didn't have any. For years, he'd been borrowing stock from other jewellers when the auditors were around, and happily nicking the cash.'

Does the proposal bear any relation to the reality of your business? The investor will want to know. One of the country's leading venture capitalists is blunt: 'Telling the difference between an OK manager and an excellent manager can be difficult. But morons are easily spotted. People we don't like to see in meetings include CEOs who don't know their numbers, and CEOs who can't present a clear strategy or tell you why they have the business, or what they are going to do with it.'

Bad managers, he says, can be easy to spot. 'They don't visit customers, or even their own operations. There's one example – it has seven factories in the UK and the CEO has only visited two of them in the last two years. He has no idea of what's happening. The company is still trading, but I'm waiting...

'Bad managers control information. So if you get into a company and find no-one is allowed to know what is going on, it's a very bad sign. But it's very common.'

There's a classic sign in companies about to hit insolvency, says the VC. 'You should really worry about this one – it nearly always happens. The CEO stops talking to his colleagues; he stops walking round the building. He starts hiding – avoiding phone calls, holes up in corner offices, makes excuses to miss meetings, not answering emails.'

And any decent potential investor will discover this by the simple means of asking around. The atmosphere in the building will very often tell its own story, too.

It's a sad fact that businesses go under every day. And they often take their owners with them. Factories blow up or burn down; key employees fall fatally ill; politics, disasters, crime, and sod's law can all have an unfortunate effect on the profit & loss account. When lightning strikes from a clear blue sky, the loss adjuster may suggest you should have foreseen it in your risk assessment, but it's a rare company that has contingencies for every act of god.

More commonly, a business failure is down to the same old litany of sins and errors, all of which boil down to bad management, however much the managers insist it was bad luck or bad karma.

The British have a negative attitude to failure; while Thomas Edison saw each failed experiment as another step closer to the solution, we take a dim view of losers. Such hatred of failure constrains the entrepreneurial spirit and stops trial for fear of error.

'Risk averse' is a term hurled at the finance community by owner managers, and hurled straight back at owner managers by financiers. The legal framework doesn't help, either – US legislation is more forgiving of the entrepreneur who tries and fails, and there is mounting pressure on government to introduce something like America's Chapter 11 bankruptcy rule to the UK.

Keep in mind the old adage that you can't be a real success until you have failed twice. Try to make the failures small and quick so you get to the success ASAP.

Where are the new Merseyside entrepreneurs?

Raising money in Liverpool used to be a hassle, which more often than not led to a trip to Manchester. Now it's the lack of budding entrepreneurs rather than funders that needs to be addressed.

When Steve Bramwell upped sticks and shifted his IT firm from London to Liverpool a few years ago, he already had venture capital backing. Bramwell, a Manc who saw the cost savings (and, he insists, a wider pool of available talent) in Liverpool was considered a brave man in those days.

In reality, he picked up prime space in the centre of the city's business district for a relative song, and he's been able to grow his business, Strategic Systems Solutions, into an award-winning global company from Tithebarn Street.

However, Bramwell knows how tough it can be raising funds and encouraging start-ups in Liverpool, a city still over-dependent on the public sector. So all-consuming are the public organisations — quangos, development bodies, public sector 'partnerships', local authorities, regeneration bodies and sub-committees of sub-committees — that commercially-run operations often find themselves competing against the public sector.

Bramwell was recently approached by one of his staff who was having a child. She wanted to open her own city centre children's nursery—

one of many services lacking in the city centre — but couldn't secure any funding. He personally put in £400,000 in start-up capital, and the venture proved such a success that she was able to launch a management buy-out of the business soon after.

Thankfully, there have been significant improvements in funders' attitudes (and yes, the 'culture' badge appears to have made them more generous). Even the fanfare that surrounded the arrival of the Queen's bank, Coutts, is an indicator of changing perceptions, and more importantly further evidence that there's money to be made on the Mersey.

However, the city's public sector remains dominant, and there are not enough home-grown entrepreneurs emerging. More locals and graduates need to have the confidence to end the wage-slave cycle and create businesses of their own, and do it in the confidence that the public sector will assist, rather than place obstacles in their way.

Scott McCubbin
editor, EN magazine

chapter 3
picking a winner

reaping the rewards

Theory is all very well, but what makes the difference between a dreamer and an entrepreneur is taking action: hard graft getting the business in shape, long hours thrashing out all the permutations of the deal, getting through the negotiations and the completion meeting, which always seems to be a cliffhanger.

In 2004 there were a good list of deals done. Here are four permutations on the theme.

TJ Hughes, the Liverpool discount retailer, had been acquired by Dave Whelan of JJB Sports in April 2002 for £42.9m; JJB then ran into tough times on the stock market, and Whelan sold TJ Hughes back to its management team of chief executive George Foster and FD Andy Goody. (Foster had tried to buy the business in 2002 but had been outbid by Whelan.) Now the pair have 15% of the company, bought for £56m by equity provider PPM Ventures with the Bank of Scotland putting together a debt package. Foster and Goody are delighted: 'Our new owners don't just bring financial backing, but also tremendous experience in the retail sector.'

A very different deal was the buyout in February of Delta Fluid Products – a company in St Helens making valves and safety equipment for the oil and gas industry.

In 2002, Delta plc sold its subsidiary DFP to the management team led by chief executive Brian Travis. The deal was backed with around £6m from Close Brothers. Just 21 months later, DFP were able grow the business to the point where they could raise a total of £8.5m, with

Liverpool-based wireless technology suppliers NuBlu signed for a third round of funding, totalling £100,000 from MSIF, Barclays and their own money. Employing six now, NuBlu expect that to treble in three years.

funds from GE Commercial Finance and other sources, to buy out Close Brothers entirely; Travis and his fellow directors now have 100% of the company.

Gareth Curran of Close Brothers said: The business outperformed our original investment plan and was ahead of its contractual redemption schedule. This gave GE Commercial Finance the confidence to back the management team with a refinancing package, which enabled them to make us a highly attractive offer to fully exit the business well in advance of target.'

Another manufacturer, this one based in Crosby and working in the wireless technology sector, has achieved a good exit with a trade sale to the Italian firm SIAE Microelettronica.

Groupe Pathfinder, with a turnover of £3m and 25 staff working for founders Richard Porter and Mike Parker, had been supported, through three rounds of funding, by Merseyside Special Investment Fund; Parker and Porter built the business from scratch, with equity and mezzanine funding totalling £680,000. The sale to the Milan-based company will give MSIF a full commercial return on their investment. Said MSIF's Jerry Mobbs: 'The acquisition by a large organisation keen to grow on Merseyside is excellent news. We will continue to watch their progress with interest.'

Porter and Parker will continue with Groupe Pathfinder; they expect their workforce to double over the next two years, and turnover to reach £30m.

A machine to move straw bales doesn't sound a likely prospect for fast growth business. But Spread-Tech's design for bale spreaders – which load bales directly from stacks, saving straw, labour and time – is winning orders from farms worldwide. Michael and Clarissa Hughes set up the company in September 2003 with a £250,000 funding package from MSIF, Barclays, North West Equity Fund and their own cash. Spread-Tech's turnover is expected to hit £1m with £5 reached in three years, says Clarissa Hughes.

Ethel Austin

In early June 2004, there were whispers among the Merseyside business community that retail chain Ethel Austin was going to announce a stock market flotation. The company had, after all, been bought by its management team in 2002 for £55m, with backing from Lloyds TSB Development Capital, and had grown so fast that LDC had been able to cash in a sizable profit 18 months later, still hanging on to most of its shares.

On 11 June, the announcement was made: it was a secondary buy-out, valuing the company at £122.5m. ABN AMRO Capital backed the management team to buy LDC out (bar a 7% stake which LDC holds for a reinvestment of £5m). The management team – CEO Phil Hoskinson (*right*), FD Steve Williams, trading director Sue Tennant and retail director Ray Caroll – increased their share from 20% to 37%, and the Austin family sold its remaining 7.5% stake.

Ethel and Ronald Austin began their business in 1934 with a wool shop in Liverpool; 70 years later the stores focus on womenswear and childrenswear, at discount prices. In 2004 there were 278 stores nationwide, 2,475 employees, and to the end of August 2003, profits of £12.9m on a turnover of £153m. The HQ and 250,000 sq.ft distribution centre are in Knowsley.

Hoskinson, who joined the firm in 1975 and became chief executive in 1988, has a five year plan to open another 200 stores and create 2,500 new jobs.

He explained why they decided against the flotation:

'It came down to the fact that the VCs valued the business more highly than the stock market.'

He added: 'ABN AMRO is a significant financial institution and its support is a major vote of confidence for everyone involved in taking the business forward. It is also a recognition for our staff and, of course, for LDC which has been a vital partner in helping us get stronger as a business.'

Hoskinson: 'Make sure you have a well thought out business plan that your investors fully understand. Ensure the plan isn't prejudiced by lack of funds.'

Toby Goodman was 18 when he set up Bannerman, a low tech advertising business which has grown steadily in its first year and has got Goodman on TV already. 'Its OK to make mistakes, as long as you learn from them,' he says.

At 16, Benjamin Huthwaite came back so inspired by the world hairdressing championships in Washington DC that he left his job with celeb hairdresser Herbert and set up on his own. Now 25, Benjamin has a long list of well known customers and a best new business award.

Star entrepreneurs can spring fully formed from nowhere, or they can build a profile through years of energetic PR and self-promotion. It is usually as difficult to spot a future star as it is to pick the winner of the Grand National, where favourites rarely get to the winners' enclosure. Who, amongst these names, will hit the really big time – and when?

Sharon Hilditch, 43, has already tasted success: the latest is winning the UK-wide NatWesteverywoman Award in December 2004. Said one of the judges: 'she has a life-long appetite for entrepreneurship, enormous strength of character, and a resolve never to give up. Her passion for her business and her success make a trul inspirational role model.' Hilditch set up her business in 1995, since when Crystal Clear skincare treatments have won strings of loyal celebrity customers, from Madonna and Kate Moss to Jude Law. A severe hearing problem meant she left school with no qualifications, but that hasn't stopped her yet, nor will it in future.

If your turnover went from £550,000 to £5m in three years, it wouldn't be too much of a shock to win an award as the enterprise champion of 2004. James Roberts, boss of Urban Engineering in Southport, has plans for serious organic growth, chasing several strategic strands and winning major contracts for the design and manufacture of bicycle shelters for schools. Now 42, he did a three year course, albeit part time, at Harvard. Will that make the difference?

As a role model for ambitious entrepreneurs, Mike Gaskell *(right)* should do nicely. In 15 years he has taken Newton-le-Willows company Morris Homes from a dud with £2m sales, through three buy-outs and a close shave with the stock market, to turnover of £150m and profits of £25m. After the third buy-out in 2004 (on 1st April) Gaskell has a personal stake of 37%, with his fellow directors holding 23% between them.

Shortly after joining the housebuilding business in 1989, Gaskell was part of the management team which bought the firm from parent Riordan for £10m. 'It took us five and a half months to raise it,' says Gaskell. Quayle Monro was backer then, and has been loyal ever since, still holding a minority share of the business.

In 1997, Gaskell was approached by brokers Charterhouse who begged him to take the company to the stock market. Gaskell and his chairman Bernard Norman had doubts, but they were persuaded, and went right the way up to impact day before Gaskell decided to pull the float. The banks with money in the company wanted an exit, but gave the team time to raise money for the secondary buy-out. This time it took them 15 days to raise £37m, with 3i joining the party.

For the 2004 deal, Morris Homes was valued at £130m; 3i sold their entire 56%. 'There's a myth that floating is the panacea to all business problems. But the reality is that we would have swapped a set of loyal institutions for a new and bigger set of shareholders.'

In 2000, Morris Homes bought Allen's building division for £24m. Asked whether the deals got any easier, Gaskell shook his head. 'It was similar to the buy-out. We did a lot of due diligence our-selves to see what was in there, but the all night completion meetings were the same,' he said.

AIM for the top of the world

Merseyside's first biotech company to float on AIM was Micap. Based in Newton-le-Willows, Micap got its listing on AIM in summer 2003, raising £5.4m. Micap are specialists in microencapsulation techniques for agrochemicals

Another Merseyside company on AIM is the Vista Group, based on the Wirral. Established in 1995, the company floated on AIM in December 2003. The company's interim results to end Jan 04 showed turnover of £7m, up 16.9% on the previous year, with pretax profits up by more than 30%

John Nichols, in his mid-50s, worked his way up from the shop floor, since joining his grandfather's firm, JN Nichols, established in 1908. Nichols is now chairman, having taken over as managing director from his father in the mid-1980s. In 1999 Nichols handed over the MD's role to Gary Unsworth, and took the chairmanship.

The company's most famous brand, Vimto, has seen something of a revival in recent years and contributes about 60% of the group's profits. The company no longer makes the fruit cordial, having outsourced all its soft

The company floated on the London Stock Exchange in the 1960s, but with turnover around the £100m mark in May 2004, John Nichols announced that the board were transferring the whole of the group's share capital to the Alternative Investment Market (AIM).

'A lot of smaller companies have done the same, because I think these days the focus in the main market is on the mega corporations. On the AIM we will be a big fish in a small pond,' said Nichols.

'A lot of our investors are individuals and it appeals to them, I think, because of the lower capital gains tax, and because the shares can be passed on through inheritance tax free.'

Having completed the transfer, after a significant restructuring of the group, Nichols then announced that the board had received an offer from MD Gary Unsworth to buy the group's division, Nichols Foods, which makes coffee, chocolate and whiteners for the

After the trek to the top of the world, you might feel like a bit of a break. But having marked the event, it's back to business as usual, trudging on across the same daunting landscape, to the next goal. A flotation might take huge effort over many months, but it is only the start of a new stage in the life of the business.

vending and retail markets. Unsworth stepped down from his MD role immediately the deal was announced, and the sale went through on 5 November 2004, with a price tag of £11.3m.

The chairman had reassured the division's 350 employees in Haydock that they would all continue with the new company. Nichols added that he was confident that the group would be a more focused business as a result of the disposal.

Merseyside plcs on the official LSE list:
Park Group
Sportech
Rathbones
Johnson Service Grp
Pilkington
MDHC
Stanley Leisure
Speedy Hire

Jargon

Corporate finance has a splendid collection of slang and jargon.
Here are some of the more common terms in current use:

acquisition: when one business buys another. Can be a hostile takeover or an agreed sale. *see M&A*

AIM (Alternative Investment Market): the little brother of the LSE. Companies don't need a three year trading history to qualify and investors are eligible for EIS

angel: *see business angel*

asset: an object of value owned by your business, which can be turned into cash. Assets can be fixed, or long term – like premises; current (short term) like stock and money owing; tangible, or intangible, eg intellectual property.

asset finance: lets a business borrow money against the value of a specific asset (eg property, plant, equipment, IP, order book) using the asset itself as security. Options include sale/lease-back, leasing and hire purchase and trade finance.

bandwidth: if there is no bandwith in a management team, there is no spare management resource available.

barriers to entry: could be anything (often a cost implication) which stops a new firm entering a given market.

beauty parade: A shortlist of advisers or financiers pitching to a business.

BIMBO (buy in/management buy out) an external entrepreneur, often with VC backing, joins the management team of the target business to buy it from its owner or parent.

BINGO: buy-in growth opportunity – an MBI team raises finance to develop and grow the business.

blue sky business: a business with potential for very high growth; often slow development with high burn rate – high risk for investors.

bridge financing: temporary short term finance required to bridge the timing gap between sources of funding.

burn rate: the rate which a company loses (burns) cash. Divide the amount of cash you have left by the burn rate to see how long the cash will last.

business angel: a private individual who, having made his or her own money, goes on to invest it in other start-ups or SMEs. May also play the role of a mentor.

capital gain: the profit made by selling an asset for more than its purchase price.

caveat emptor: 'buyer beware' – the burden is on the buyer to make sure the asset for sale is fit for the purpose.

caveat venditor: 'seller beware' – the seller has a legal obligation to disclose any problems with the asset. In theory, charging sellers with responsibility only requires them to be expert in their own business; buyers would have to be expert in every business.

company buy-back: a company buying back its own shares from the shareholders.

debt finance: and or other debt facilities; interest is payable at an agreed rate and agreed intervals (eg monthly or quarterly).

demerger: business splits into two or more separate companies, eg as the result of an MBO, or a failed M&A.

drag along: rights in a company's Articles of Association that allow the majority shareholder to drag along the minority shareholders in the sale of the business. *see tag along*

due diligence: detailed company analysis done once a deal is agreed in principle, to discover the financial, commercial and legal health of the company and management team.

early stage funding: *see seed finance*

earnings per share: profit after tax divided by the number of shares. A company may decide to reinvest some of the profit in the company before dividing the remainder between shareholders. A useful tool in determining share and corporate value of plcs.

EBITDA: earnings before interest, tax, depreciation and amortisation.

equity: equity investors own a business (the shares in it). If the business prospers the equity partners share the profits but they also share the risk if the company fails.

equity gap: the size bracket of deals where businesses find it hardest to interest investors. Typically between £250,000 and £2 million – although the upper limit is steadily rising.

exit: when investors and management decide the time is right to realise a return on their investment.

exit strategy: the various options for realising an investment in the business, which could include a secondary buy-out, flotation, or trade sale.

factoring and invoice discounting: outsourcing the collection of money owed; the factor or invoice discounter advances money as soon as an invoice is issued then recovers the debt from the customer.

first-round funding: funds available to start-ups, which – on the basis of a good business plan – receive financial support to take their idea or product to market.

flotation: listing a company on the stock market, by offering shares to the general public. *see IPO*

FSA: Financial Services Authority, the regulator for the financial industry.

FTSE: Financial Times Stock Exchange – the list of share prices and movements on the London Stock Exchange and AIM.

funding cocktail: the mix of equity, debt, mezzanine and asset finance that can combine to fund a deal.

gap funding: funding for deals that fall into the equity gap (£0.25m – £3m); or the last piece of the financial jigsaw that makes up any deal.

gearing: the ratio of debt to ordinary share capital – a company with a high proportion of debt is highly geared.

good leaver/bad leaver: contractual terms on which a director leaves the company with rewards or penalties.

guarantee: a pledge to fulfill the debt or responsibilities of another person or company, if they fail to carry them out.

see warranties

hamster wheel: a business which will not reach critical mass; where the managers runs around, getting tired and frustrated.

hostile bid: bid to takeover company not supported by the target company's directors. *see agreed bid*

IBO (institutional buy out): a buy-out in which the institution – usually a venture capitalist or bank – acquires a majority stake in the target company.

information rights: a right to gain information about a company (eg attending board meetings), usually granted to venture capitalists investing in private companies.

intellectual property (IP): intangible assets of a company, eg brands, trademarks, copyright or design right. IP rights protect the owner from unauthorised copying – but it may require legal action to do so.

internal rate of return: *see IRR*

investment philosophy: the rationale behind a venture capitalist or private equity fund's decision to invest – or not – in a certain type of company. Some may not invest in particular types of company (eg dotcoms) whilst others will be sector specific, eg early-stage technology companies.

invoice discounting: *see factoring*

IPO (initial public offering): American jargon for a flotation, increasingly used in the UK.

IRR: internal rate of return set by investors to calculate the cost to the investee company of the equity investment; used as a key criterion of the company's annual performance.

junk bond: a high yield, high risk bond, often issued for high value leveraged buy-outs and takeovers. Particularly suited to investors who relish the risk aspect; dividends and risks are high.

leveraged buy-out: a buy-out using a high ratio of debt to equity.

listed company: refers to a plc that is listed on a Stock Exchange.

management buy-in: an external management team buys in to a target company.

management buy-out: the management team buys the company it is running – eg when the company founder retires, or when a plc sells a subsidiary.

MBI: *see management buy in*

MBO: *see management buy out*

mergers and acquisitions (M&A): a phrase describing the whole range of activities associated with buy and selling companies.

mezzanine finance: may be part of a funding cocktail, it carries higher interest than a term loan; the lender can opt for a small equity stake, or a lump sum premium on exit.

net profit: the difference between sales revenues and total costs.

newco: the new company formed through a buy-out, start-up, merger or demerger.

non-executive director: a board-level director, without responsibility for day to day running of the company; mandatory for all plcs and for venture-backed companies. Brings impartiality and a broader view to company proceedings. Just as liable as executive directors if things go wrong.

OFEX: an unregulated matched bargain market established in 1995 by JP Jenkins, authorised by the FSA. About 200 companies are listed on OFEX, mostly small, young companies with a high-tech bent. Admission to OFEX is quicker and much cheaper than AIM or the main lists, but liquidity is poor and stocks are high risk.

official list: the London Stock Market's main list (as opposed to AIM or OFEX).

OMB: owner managed business

pathfinder: market research to proposed investors for a planned flotation. Carries details of the float to gauge viability and response to the project.

P/E: price/earnings ratio – a means of determing the value of a business through a multiple of earnings. A p/e of

3 would be a low price; a p/e of 30 would be a highly valued business, although what is a high P/E in one sector may be low in another.

PEG: price earnings growth factor, calculated by dividing a company's prospective P/E ratio by the estimated future growth rate in earnings per share of the company. A PEG of 1 or lower is attractive to buyers.

plc: a public limited company (not always quoted on the stock market).

portfolio: a range of investments held by an individual or a venture capitalist.

post-money valuation: valuation after the investment. If investors put $0.5m into a $3m pre-money company, the post-money valuation is $3.5m. The percentage of the company given to the investors is based on the post-money valuation; here, £500k / $3.5m = 14%.

pre-money valuation: the valuation or total price of a company before the investment.

private equity: private equity capital invested in businesses that hasn't come from the public (stock) markets. Also the term that describes the industry that has developed around such investments.

PTP: pre-tax profit. *see EBITDA*

quoted company: a company with its share price quoted on a stock exchange index (eg TechMARK, NASDAQ). *See listed company*

return on investment (ROI): the total percentage increase in capital over the life of the investment.

ring master: an intermediary (eg corporate finance adviser) who coordinates the fundraising process.

risk capital: *see venture capital*

secondary buy out (2BO): the institutional investor exits, after their role in the original buy-out, and sells their share in the business on to another investor, or back to the original shareholders.

seed capital: funding provided by a venture capitalist or specialist equity fund used to finance start up and early stage businesses.

share capital: *see equity*

SME: small-medium sized enterprise

structured finance: collection of all debt instruments used to fund an acquisition.

syndicate: a group of investors or lenders joining in an opportunity.

tag along: gives minority shareholders the right to join in with the majority shareholders on the sale of their shares.

takeover bid: an attempt to buy shares in a target company – often at a higher price than their market value – in order to gain a controlling interest in the said company.

TechMARK: an index of technology stocks launched in 1999 by the London Stock Exchange. For companies on the Official List committed to technological innovation. It includes biotechnology companies as well as internet stocks and software companies.

terminal value (TV): the formula for calculating the value of a company when sold – TV= P(1+r)t, where P = initial sum invested, r = interest rate and t = time invested.

trade sale: sale of one business to another; one of the main exit routes.

venture capital: also known as risk capital. Private equity capital available for businesses, usually from a mix of institutional funds. Venture capitalists are also called VCs.

VIMBO or **VRMBO**: Vendor investing buy out – where the company selling part of its business to a buy-out team reinvests in the newco (often cheaper or less divisive than other forms of disposal)

war chest: money in hand to fund acquisitions

warranties: promises and guarantees that a vendor makes to a purchaser about assets, performance and liabilities of the company. Often secured against personal assets, with a financial cap, and tied in to an earn-out for the vendor.

getting help

DEEP END

Steve Stuart Partnership
Deals from idea to completion
Contact Steve Stuart
Steve.Stuart@tsspllp.co.uk
0151 243 0584

Bibby Factors (NW)
Unlocking asset value for SMEs
www.bibbyfinancialservices.com
0151 479 7600

DWF
Utterly commercial legal service
Contact Philip Whitehurst
Philip.Whitehurst@dwf.co.uk
0151 907 3000

**Government Office
North West**
eu&merseyside: the Objective
One programme
www.euandmerseyside.org
0151 224 6441

MSIF
Funding for Merseyside SMEs
Contact Geraldine McEntegart
Geraldine.McEntegart@msif.co.uk
0151 236 4040

Midas Capital
Fund management
Contact: Simon Edwards
www.midascapital.co.uk
info@midascapital.co.uk
0151 906 2450

The Mersey Partnership
Investing in Merseyside
Contact Mark Basnett
mark.basnett@merseyside.org.uk
0151 227 2727

CAPITAL OF CULTURE 2008
Liverpool Culture Company
Creating the 2008 Capital of Culture
www.liverpoolculture.com
0151 233 1360

BUSINESS SUPPORT
BusinessLiverpool
Creating a world class city for
business
0151 288 6677
info@businessliverpool.co.uk
www.businessliverpool.co.uk
One-stop-shop for local entrepreneurs and would-be investors, LBC
partners the local Business Link,
Chamber of Commerce, City Council
and Greater Merseyside Enterprise,
coordinating its partners financial
services, plus its own Financial
Assistance to Business scheme. Also
provides information on the local
economy, workforce etc., runs property searches, and promotes
Liverpool as a business destination
both nationally and internationally.

Business Link
0845 330 0151
www.gme.org.uk
Greater Merseyside s Business Link
gives advice and support to help start
up and grow businesses finding
finance, plus access to independent
advice from the professionals, including 40% off their fees.

Chambers of Commerce
Legal help, grant, aid and incentives
advice and general help and support
for local businesses. Liverpool
Chamber runs the Thrive and Survive
scheme with MSIF.
Halton
0151 423 6606
www.haltonchamber.org.uk
Knowsley
0151 477 1356
www.knowsleychamber.org.uk
Liverpool
0151 227 1234
www.liverpoolchamber.org.uk
St Helens
01744 742 000
www.sthelenschamber.com

Sefton
01704 531 710
www.seftonchamber.com
Wirral
0151 647 8899
www.wirralchamber.org.uk

Infopool
0845 145 1115
www.infopool.co.uk
The gateway to a wealth of business information and support services. Part of BusinessLiverpool, Infopool also boasts a comprehensive electronic directory.

Motivating Merseyside Businesses to Innovate (MMBI)
0151 632 8881 www.mmbi.org.uk
Aimed at technology-based SMEs based on Merseyside, MMBI can help you further your business by developing new ideas, products and services through accessing networks, technologies and funding. Funded by the European Regional Development Fund and the NWDA, it taps into specialist knowledge at the University of Liverpool and John Moores, and teams up with both Business Link for Greater Merseyside and a range of mentors.

Muslim Enterprise Development Service
0151 709 6567
info@muslimenterprise.co.uk
www.muslimenterprise.co.uk

INWARD INVESTMENT
The Mersey Partnership
0151 227 2727
www.merseyside.org.uk
Promotes Merseyside to inward investors and tourists, whilst carrying out research on the region, and promoting local businesses as part of the regional package .

THE UNIVERSITIES
Aside from the improved business courses they now run, the universities are a great source of research and business information, and have a number of research and development projects on the go.

John Moores University
0151 231 3830 www.livjm.ac.uk
The Business Improvement
Programme provides training and support, from business planning and financial management to language skills and
a specialised mentoring programme.
Funding from the Learning Skills
Council of Greater Merseyside and
the European Social Fund also means
that there are 80% reductions for
eligible Merseyside SMEs.

University of Liverpool
0845 0700 064 www.liv.ac.uk
Includes the Centre for Business
Management, which specialises in e-
business, e-learning and entrepreneurship, and creating real commercial
start-ups on graduation.

Liverpool Community College
Business Training Centre
0151 709 3079 www.liv-coll.ac.uk

Hope University College
0151 291 3856 www.hope.ac.uk

GOVERNMENT OFFICES
Office for the North West
0151 224 6415
www.euandmerseyside.org
Administers Objective One funding

RDA
Northwest Development Agency
01925 400 100 www.nwda.co.uk
Provides strategic leadership to the
region, and a number of different
funds, developing business competitiveness and extending the region s
skills base.

FUNDING
Business Investment Scheme
0161 832 7603 www.nwbis.co.uk
A NWDA fund, investing in Objective
2 areas, including Halton, with funding
of up to £500,000 from a total pot of
£17.5 million.

British Venture Capital Association
/www.bvca.co.uk/

Culture Finance Loan Fund

Micro credit for the creative industries in the North West
0161 839 6041
info@culturefinance.co.uk
www.culturefinance.co.uk

Grant for Research & Development

01925 400 468
www.dti.gov.uk/r-d
Replacing the DTI SMART scheme, this is not just local to Merseyside, but invests across the UK. A primary provider of development funds for innovation, from £20,000 to £500,000.

Liverpool Seed Fund

Contact Steve Nesbitt
Liverpool Ventures
0151 236 4040
A new seed fund, providing very early stage risk capital to knowledge-based high risk start ups and pre-start ups in incubation. With a total fund of just under £27 million, Liverpool Seed Fund will provide three stages of fund-ing: Proof of Concept funding (£40,000 - £50,000) for viability and market testing, Commercialisation (up to £250,000) for manufacturing proto-types and early sales, and 1st Round Venture Capital — development finance of up to £500,000.

Merseyside Special Investment Fund

0151 236 4040
www.msif.co.uk
MSIF advises and supports businesses, right through from the early ideas stage to the three pots of money it administrates. The Small Firms Fund provides loans of up to £100,000, while the Mezzanine fund offers loans of up to £1 million, and the Venture Fund a maximum of £2 million. Combinations of monies from the three different pots are also up for grabs. It also runs the Family Business programme, Business Owners Support Service (BOSS), a Mentors programme and I-BUY, the Intelligent Buying Programme.

North West Equity Fund

01925 759 246

www.nwef.co.uk

The regional Venture Capital Fund of the Year aims to try and plug the equity gap with a total of £35 million to invest, in tranches of up to £250,000.

North West Seed Fund

0161 828 5221

www.nwseedfund.com

£4.5 million to invest, with a total investment each time of £100,000, plus business building support and mentoring.

Rising Stars Fund

01772 270 582

www.enterprise-ventures.co.uk

Again the NWDA is a majority investor this fund has tranches of up to £500,000 to invest from a £19 million fund, in high growth early-stage technology start-ups.

TEChINVEST

01925 400 301

www.techinvest.org

Run by the NWDA, TEChINVEST matches companies looking for finance with wealthy investors looking for somewhere to put their cash...

INCUBATORS

Music Bias

0151 330 4192 www.musicbias.org

Support service, helping Merseyside-based music ventures get off the ground, from business planning to grants advice and take-off.

International Centre for Digital Content (ICDC)

0151 231 5129

www.icdc.org.uk

Pushing Liverpool to the front of the digital agenda, ICDC provides sector-based research, using it to fuel its teaching and production sides.

ACME

0151 233 4632

www.merseysideacme.com

The strategic development agency for Merseyside s creative sector, providing access to advice, business development services and finance.

MerseyBio
0151 795 4100 www.merseybio.com
Developing the region s life sciences sector through start-up and incubation support, assistance to SMEs and attracting inward investment.

BUSINESS PRESS
Local and regional business press is the freshest source of news and information.

Daily Post
0151 472 2319
www.icliverpool.com
Liverpool Echo
0151 472 2451
www.icliverpool.com

en Magazine
www.excelpublishing.co.uk

North West Business Insider
0161 907 9709
www.newsco.co.uk

BBC Radio Merseyside
0151 708 5500
www.bbc.co.uk/radiomerseyside

PROFESSIONALS
Lots of different criteria will affect your decision to choose a certain firm; not least the range of skills on offer. Consider whether you want to be a tiny client for a huge firm, or you want to be the big fish client to a smaller, local firm

Professional Liverpool
Is the central contact for over 60 professional firms in Liverpool.
www.professionaliverpool.com

All revenue from the sale of The Culture of Capital will be donated to Emmaus

Giving people a bed — and a reason to get out of it

Emmaus Communities offer homeless men and women a home, work and the chance to rebuild their self-respect in a supportive, community environment.

Companions, as residents are known, work full time refurbishing donated furniture and household goods and selling them in the community shop. The community aims to become self-sufficient through this activity.

www.emmaus.org.uk

Merseyside Special Investment Fund